The
Medicine Woman
Inner Guidebook

Carol Bridges

The
Medicine Woman
Inner Guidebook

**A Woman's Guide to
Her Unique Powers
Using the
Medicine Woman Tarot Deck
Created by Carol Bridges**

U.S. GAMES SYSTEMS, INC.
Publishers   Stamford, CT 06902 USA

All illustrations, including cover, by Carol Bridges

Edited and designed by Jean Hoots

Library of Congress Catalog Card Number: 91-75047

ISBN 0-88079-512-3

10 9 8 7 6 5

Printed in the USA

U.S. GAMES SYSTEMS, INC.
179 Ludlow Street
Stamford, CT 06902 USA

*to the Grandmothers
and Grandfathers
and my tribe of spiritual family*

Contents

Using the Medicine Woman Tarot Deck

Disclaimer

The purpose of *The Medicine Woman Inner Guidebook* is to inspire your own search and discovery of the truth that lives inside yourself. It is also a sharing of my own personal journey and of the concepts that have best served my own empowerment. Many of the teachings in this book can be found, though in different words, in documents of the great religions of the world. There are other books, available to anyone who seeks to find them, that elucidate the teachings in greater detail. This book was never meant to be the last word on my own or anyone else's spirituality. All advice and suggestions, whether spiritual, health-related or psychological, are offered with the sincere hope that the reader will take them into her own being and make judgments from her own inner wisdom.

The complicated legal and medical system of our present society makes it imperative that the author and the publisher state that neither will have liability or responsibility to any person or entity with respect to any loss or damage caused or alleged to be caused directly or indirectly by the information contained in *The Medicine Woman Inner Guidebook*. In my heart, I feel saddened that such warnings and disclaimers are needed. It is my hope that someday we can all live in a society where we take responsibility for ourselves and do our best to help and cooperate with all beings.

This book will not make you a Medicine Wo/man. You must make the choices and take the actions which lead to your own evolution. May this book assist you along the way to the full realization of your potential and power.

The Medicine Woman Tarot deck and *The Medicine Woman Inner Guidebook* are not meant to represent any particular Native American tradition. Instead, I have chosen to image in a new reality of "nativeness" which draws from the essence of many tribal ways. I am native to North America and my people are of this land. The lessons and images contained herein are to inspire a conscious union with this land and to honor all native people who have so loved Earth through their sacred ways and traditions.

Introduction

The Medicine Woman Inner Guidebook imagines a new reality of tribal ways based on native awareness of the land and drawing wisdom from many sacred traditions. The premises on which *The Medicine Woman Inner Guidebook* is based are as follows.

"Medicine" is used in the Native American sense of the word, as in "Medicine Man" or "Medicine Woman." Medicine means healing. It is a force that makes correction in that which was out of balance. I use the words "Medicine Woman" rather than "Medicine Man" because the medicine of this book is to assist in restoring balance within society and individuals, and it is the feminine aspect which is currently lacking. Whether you are male or female, this book is meant to bring the feminine healing aspect of you into realization.

A Medicine Woman gains her power on the path of life. Through her interactions with creation, she chooses her destiny.

There is a voice-within-you that, in all situations, knows your correct answer and speaks it. Through this book you are guided to listen.

There is a body-knowledge telling you at all times what to eat, where to go, when to move. You will discover this dance.

The sexual energy, so compelling a force, through your

practices draws to you exactly what you need and desire.

The hands that now work for you also heal. As you align your desires with the highest good for all, you become a channel, a woman of good medicine.

Life is your power. The Creator is you, bringing life into the world through the patterns of your thinking, the images of your mind. Woman, womb of creation, these are your powers!

To use this book, you must become friends with it. It is not like other books. It speaks not only to the intellect, but to the body, emotions, and spirit. You must write in it, speak to it, cry about it, laugh with yourself. All of the characters depicted are roles you play, people in your life, archetypal forces, and medicine helpers rolled into one. At the same time, they depict a path of life, the laws of manifestation, the biochemical interaction of cells, the evolution of humanity, and your daily encounters. There are many levels through which these people—the Medicine Woman Tarot—will be working with you.

In the tarot deck, there are twenty-two Major Arcana, which I call the Great Mystery. The fifty-six Minor Arcana are called the Four Powers in the Medicine Woman Tarot deck. The Minor Arcana have traditionally comprised four suits: pentacles or coins, wands or staves, swords, and cups. In the Medicine Woman Tarot the four suits, or powers, are called Stones (coins), Pipes (wands), Arrows (swords), and Bowls (cups). Each power has ten numbered cards, and four cards that correspond to the court cards of traditional tarot decks: apprentice (page), totem (knight), lodge (queen), and exemplar (king).

Cards 0 through 21 show the path a life follows from birth to fulfillment. The first eight cards tell you how to manifest a thing into being.

0 Seed: Plant the seed idea.

1 Resources: Take stock of earthly resources.

2 Seeker: Look within for spiritual resources.

3 Bounty: Practice contentment by nurturing and appreciating what you have already been given.

4 Command: Take command of that which needs to be changed.

5 Peacemaker: Present your idea to the world.

6 Ecstasy: Maintain your inner/outer balance.

7 Warrior: Take note of your achievement.

The nervous system receives, integrates, and transmits knowledge, and the consciousness goes through these same three stages to accomplish major life changes. You have been programmed by DNA in every cell to spiral onward until, as your awareness increases, you are more and more able to take over the job of programming yourself. In other words, you are meant to become a Goddess, a creator of your own reality.

The beginning of this awareness of self-creation, I call the medicine path, and you who walk upon it, a Medicine Woman. You are beginning to *make real*, to "real"-ize, the powers of life at your command. You are *responsible* to make changes in your world, society, and self. On the path, you enable your self to become ever more able to respond powerfully to every situation and to create with it the life you need.

The Medicine Woman Tarot is a guide to help you on this journey of responsibility. The cards will come to life in your meditations and will become spirit friends to share your joys and sort through your sorrows. The exercises will help you put what you learn into action. The visualizations will give your body/mind the images to lead you to your own greatness. How quickly, how thoroughly, how happily you travel the path depends on you, for "time" is the only perception that prevents you from being there now.

In the text, you will find that I have often used the spelling "hir" to indicate both male and female gender. The common pronouns "him, her, he, she" are used occasionally for clarity.

I have also oriented the drawings and references throughout the book and deck primarily toward women. This is not to exclude men from the lessons, but to heal a cultural situation where most everything is oriented toward men. It is hoped that any man reading this book will understand the need for this healing. *The Medicine Woman Inner Guidebook* attempts to be good medicine. Part of its purpose is to supply powerful images where there has been a lack of power. Consequently, a male is the main character in the suit of Bowls, the energy of which is love and devotion. It is here that male power is currently denied by the technological culture.

In all other Minor Arcana drawings, a woman is the main character. It is my purpose to empower women in areas where their power has been denied. The archetypal characters of the Major Arcana are both male and female. Where a stronger yang (masculine) force is called for, I have used a male. But it must be understood that the yang force is within each human being and does not belong only to those of one body structure.

I feel that the division of humans into two sexes is arbitrary. We exist in a spectrum of sexuality and body types. There are extremes at either end, but most of us stand somewhere in between. A Medicine Woman is any person who has recognized and actualized hir female powers, acting with intuition, love, and creative force to make this world "home" for all generations to come.

Capitalization of a common word designates the cosmic or greatest aspect of the word. For example, "Self" with a capital "S" represents the High Self or divine portion of your being. "Self" with a small "S" is the personality or everyday self.

I have used "God," "Goddess," "Great Spirit", and "Creator" to designate the power behind all that is. Each word depicts a different quality of the one Great Being. To me, "Being" is the perfect God-word because it implies both an entity and/or a state of being. It implies the mystery. And though this mystery may appear to us in any form, it will always be something we cannot quite grasp with our rational minds. Do not let my choice of words interfere with your intuitive knowing of the truth.

The Circle Continues

Once upon a time, long ago, the People of High Consciousness observed that the world was beginning to be overrun
by people unable to perceive the Wholeness. There was a
danger that the almighty powers that were meant to be
used for the good of all would annihilate the planet if the
knowledge of the laws of nature were to be known by those
without a love for her.

So the High Ones, in their cleverness, condensed all of
these Laws and Great Teachings into images that fit on
seventy-eight cards. And they gave the cards to wanderers
whom no one would suspect of carrying the ancient wisdom. We called the wanderers "gypsies" and the deck of
cards "the tarot," a word that means:

ROTA:	The Wheel, or Circle
ORAT:	Speaks
TORA:	The Law
ATOR:	Of Nature

The gypsies played the cards of life as they traveled, and
through the images, the Truths were passed to minds that
were open to receive them.

To the receptive minds who gazed upon the gypsies'
tarot, there came inspiration to walk in greater harmony,
coming into conscious union with Creation. Through time,

the Earth has given every land a tribe of people who see wholeness. The Whole People live the knowledge that all creatures are their sisters and brothers. The winds and rains, the sun and moon, the rocks and waters—these, too, they understand to be their relatives. Through their visions, they have come to see that this Way is the keeping of Paradise upon the land.

The Whole People have built circles of stones to remind them of the circles of life. They have called these circles Medicine Wheels. They have told stories of the powers of all directions, recognizing the consciousness that every being must pass through as they travel through these powers around the Wheel of Life. Always, the Whole People have seen that what is taken must be given. What is reaped must be sown. And the circle of life continues.

Yet, still upon the Earth there are ones who do not see. These People of No Vision use their eyes as though disconnected from their hearts. This separation has caused a great sickness, the effects of which we are experiencing now.

It is time for Good Medicine. It is time once again to look to the Wheel of Life which speaks the Laws of Nature. It is time to find your own vision of Wholeness, and to learn the steps which are yours to take in the Earth Dance. This the Grandmothers and the Grandfathers cry out. This was their prayer as they called us to Earth. This was their prayer as they died and were born in us. This is the call we hear now.

The People of High Consciousness observe that the world is beginning to be overrun by people unable to perceive the Wholeness. There is a danger that the almighty powers meant to be used for the good of all will annihilate the planet if the knowledge of the Laws of Nature are to be known by those without a love for Her.

The Medicine Woman Tarot may pass your way. If you are a High One, you will learn from the images the secrets

7

that will maintain the Wholeness of Life. You will become a Keeper of Earth, honoring all life that has come before you. You will create a circle of stones to remind you. As you live, so will life return to you. The Powers will become your friends. The Circle of Life will continue.

The Basics

Each aspect of your being is involved in all you do. Your body follows the instructions it receives through the image you hold in your mind. The emotions evoked by your images are the fires that energize you, the fuel that moves your body toward that which has been imagined. Emotion is evoked motion, e[voked]motion. Your mind is the movie director. It decides the images you choose to allow to guide you. The body simply gives form to this process. It embodies your thinking. It gives shape to the patterns in your mind.

Images speak to you constantly. The words you hear yourself saying are telling you about the images you hold in your mind. If you listen to yourself, you will discover the inner movie that constantly becomes your life. Are you pleased with the script? Do you like the roles you have everyone playing? If not, perhaps it is time for good medicine.

The Medicine Woman Tarot is a tool to help you change your mind and thus your body, your life, and your world. The images on the cards are used to heighten your awareness of the characters who live inside you. Often they will remind you of friends and relations. The cards are also yourself. In truth, all your friends and relations live inside of you in the roles that create your personal movie. Everything you see outside yourself is merely a reflection of what

9

is happening inside. This is the realization that brings you into connection with all things. This is the realization that brings your power.

Everything you change within yourself also becomes changed in the outside world. The medicine path you walk each day brings you to consciousness of the events taking place within/around you and gives you the choice to change for the good of the whole.

As you become friends with the tarot characters, they will begin to speak to you about just what "the good of the whole" is and how you might take steps toward that good in your life. The tarot teachers on the cards know all about life and are not likely to be surprised by any of your feelings or failings. They have, after all, been helping people for many centuries. They are the archetypal forces of love and wisdom.

How to Use the Cards

With each Great Mystery card of the Medicine Woman Tarot is a description that includes the following.

A **number** and its **meaning**. This system of giving meaning to numbers allows them to speak to you when you see them showing up in your life. In this way, they can deliver timely messages very quickly.

The **traditional name** of the tarot character. The name will usually depict a role that you play and that others play in your life. The character shown knows how to play that role the best way it can be played. The characters are thus archetypal. They are similar to a superstar in their particular role. Each one has been playing the same part in the cosmic drama since the beginning of time.

The **Medicine Woman energy** that flows through the character. This is the quality about which the card is trying to tell you.

An **affirmation** to help you open to the power of this energy within you. By repeating the affirmation often, you are rehearsing, so that when you need to play this role in your life, you will do it well.

An explanation, called **The Card Speaks**, of the meaning of the card by the tarot character itself. This will give you a better idea of the character's personality. The personality will become richer every time you meditate on the card or play the role.

Self-questioning statements to help you find the energy of each card within yourself. It is best to write your answers in a journal.

An **exercise** to create a situation in which you will *experience* the energy of the card. Reading about the meaning of the card is merely intellectual entertainment. Experience brings the knowledge through the senses.

A **meditation** to allow you to receive input from the card. The image may change to affect more dramatically *you* individually. Simply let the card take the form most meaningful to your relationship with it. The card will become an inner teacher.

A **visualization** to help you see yourself in the perfection of the card's energy. This brings the teacher's wisdom into your daily life.

The **astrological sign** associated with the card. For those of you who have knowledge of astrology, this will help to integrate that knowledge with the Medicine Woman Tarot.

Foods and colors are sometimes suggested as they also affect consciousness. You can experiment in order to discover how certain foods and colors cause different moods or feeling tones. You may see how they can change your mental state as well.

I strongly suggest that you go through the book, lesson by lesson, getting to know the cards and yourself before attempting to do any tarot "readings" in order to predict future events. You will find by doing so that you unleash the power within you to create the future you really desire rather than simply having to feel yourself to be a pawn in someone else's game. The Medicine Woman Tarot can be a profound spiritual tool if you use it for Self-understanding and to aid in your ability to make choices that bring balance and wholeness to the circle of life.

You are the magic in the cards. Let the cards be the key that opens the door to your higher being.

How to Affirm, Visualize, and Meditate

Affirmation: This is a positive statement. The more you say the affirmation inwardly or out loud, the more your subconscious will begin to adopt it as fact. Then your being will begin to act in the positive manner suggested by the affirmation. Just run it through your mind as often as possible. It also helps to write the affirmation down and place it at eye level in a spot you will pass by several times a day.

Visualization: This is a process of picturing in your mind's eye something that you wish to come true. It presupposes that you have already tuned in to yourself prior to the visualization to make sure that what you are going to picture is right for you.

If you have trouble visualizing or feel that you "have no imagination," you can enhance your imaging qualities by first gazing open-eyed at a picture or photograph of a simple, inspiring scene. The scene should be one that leads your eye down a path, through a doorway or gate, or around a corner of some kind. In other words, there should be a sense that you could walk right into the picture and go to some secret place.

Sit quietly. Gaze at the picture. Close your eyes and remember it in your mind's eye. Open your eyes. Gaze at the picture. Close your eyes. Make your inner vision more clear. Open your eyes. Gaze at any details your mind left out. Close your eyes. Visualize the scene again. You will find that your imaging-in power is much greater than you expected. Do this exercise as often as necessary.

Then close your eyes, envision the scene. Smell the smells that would be there. Feel the weather. Allow yourself to travel the path and go beyond the scene. Or open the door, go through the gate. The only control to exercise is to keep your mind focused on going farther into what you are creating as opposed to thinking about what to make for supper or dwelling on some other everyday rational thought.

You will learn how to visualize better and better as you do the exercises, meditations, and visualizations suggested throughout the book.

Meditation: There are many forms of meditation. Several will be experienced in later exercises in this book. The main method to understand at this point is that you must be willing to systematically put aside your everyday thoughts while in the process of meditating. They will pass by your mind, but do not stop to dwell on them. Instead, follow the directions given in the specific meditation for each card.

13

Meditation does require discipline. It is an act of power on your part. But you have what it takes to do it. Practice brings results far beyond your imagining because your current level of imagining is (if you do not meditate) much less than it could be.

Be patient with yourself as you learn to still the everyday mind. You will achieve results. Each lesson of the tarot will take you deeper and deeper into the great mystery of cosmic consciousness, the mind of God of which you are a part. Have faith in yourself and read on.

The Great Mystery: The Major Arcana

The Medicine Woman Energies of the Great Mystery

0 **Seed :** The Seed Being Carried by the Wind

1 **Resources:** The Resourceful One Using the Tools at Hand

2 **Seeker:** Seeker of the Light Within

3 **Bounty:** Bountiful Earth Mother

4 **Command:** Taking Command for the Good of All

5 **Peacemaker:** The Peacemaker Interfacing with the World

6 **Ecstasy:** The Lovers, Finding the Spirit Within, Unite with Ecstasy

7 **Warrior:** Victorious Warrior

8 **Healing:** Healing Power

9 **Guide:** The Guide on the Path Up the Mountain

10 **Harvest:** The Season's Harvest

0 SEED

Number and Meaning: 0, Openness to flow

Traditional Name: The Fool

Medicine Woman Energy: The Seed Being Carried by the Wind

Affirmation: "All the power that ever was or will be exists in the here and now. I am therefore ready and willing to risk the loss of what I have been and move on to what I can become. I am the power to begin."

The Card Speaks: "I am the Fool, a Seed Being Carried by the Wind. I am the first step in the process of manifestation. I am the idea that inspires life. I am inexperienced, yet within me lies the plan for my perfect unfoldment. To me, there is no time like the present in which to begin my journey.

"I carry my memories, my talents, my hopes, my dreams, my fears, and concerns in the bowl of my self, just as you carry these within the cells of your body. I carry the seed of Self into every adventure. My fears summon me to prepare and make ready to overcome any dangers that might be ahead. The Light of the Sun illuminates my way.

"By Earth, mother of all creation, I am nourished. Through movement and change I grow. My path is revealed as I walk on."

Exercise: This week, do something you have always wanted to do.

Meditation: Imagine that you are a fool, going on an inner journey. Read the instructions, "Beginning the Journey: A

Map of Consciousness," on the next few pages. Then find a comfortable, quiet place to sit with your spine straight, and follow the path in your mind to meet your Guiding Presence. When you sense a contact has been made, ask to be presented with information regarding the Seed which your life is carrying into the world.

Visualization: Creating the image in as much detail and color as possible, envision yourself bravely taking the next step in your spiritual journey. The step may be anything from cleaning the house to organizing a political action group. The truth is only within you.

Astrological Sign: Uranus

Foods: Foods that stimulate activity often have caffeine, a substance not healthful in large amounts. Try the following tea as a substitute.

Fool's Tea: Boil 1 cup fresh clear water containing a piece of ginger root, 2 whole cloves, 4 cardamon seeds, 3 black peppers, and 1/2 cinnamon stick for 10 minutes, then add 1 teaspoon of any good strong herbal tea. Allow to steep 10 minutes. Add 1/2 cup of milk and heat until warm enough for drinking.

Diet is an important aspect of being able to move into altered states of awareness and experience the deeper levels of relaxation and higher insight that are suggested in this book. The healthier you are, the easier it is for your psyche to free itself from bodily concerns.

Colors: Surround yourself with a clear, light yellow or with glorious dawn hues. Try meditating on the Seed at sunrise. The Seed is awakening. Go out early in the morning to a dewy meadow or a small stream. Let yourself softly gaze without thinking. The feelings that will come are the essence of the Fool or Seed energy.

Beginning the Journey:
A Map of Consciousness

Whenever one is traveling in new territory, it is helpful to have a map. It is the same with the pathways to the inner Self. Eventually, all roads lead to the One Perfection, but just as one might prefer to take a scenic, winding country road rather than a concrete superhighway, the choice of your path depends on the kind of adventure you would most enjoy.

I have mapped out a road to the dwelling place of the Inner Guide, a helping force that lives within each person. This Guide may appear as a Medicine Woman, or as a figure from biblical times, or in any number of ways depending on the associations contained in your intellectual storehouse. You might find it easiest to think of the Guide as a part of yourself, yet able to be distinct and different in order to communicate more easily with your personality. Yet the Guide is also more than "you." Hir presence brings you new information and hir love far surpasses your own.

We are all beings much larger than we think. Just as in the diagram of the Goddess Information (page 21), I see us being a large cosmic energy pattern. On the outer limits, if you were to look from o v e r h e a d, we are beings gently moved by the planetary fields and celestial influences as described through astrology. The lines of force or planetary vibrations become finer patterns of energy and are seen as archetypal personifications of various qualities. These figures of beings are those that appear in profound dreams, visions, and meditations on the tarot characters as they make contact with our individual psyches. Then at an even closer level to us, there are the Guiding Beings. The Guides are the gathering together of inspiration/information into a

19

personal form that entices us forward on our spiritual journey. All of these forces can remain unconscious and still work. You don't have to know about them in order for them to be there. However, this is like having a family whom you never see because you have locked yourself in a small room of a very large house. The Guides and archetypes are your Spiritual Family. You are now preparing to meet them for the first time and to bring them into conscious relationship with yourself.

Within the center of these guiding forces, at the heart of the energy pattern, is the force field known as the Self. Around that which is your physical being, you carry a cloud of beliefs, desires, feelings, wishes, memories, thoughts, attitudes, programs, longings, and expectations—the total accumulation of all you have ever done, thought, or said. As you complete interactions and change your ways of thinking or behaving, windows open to the Larger Self (the world of Guides and Archetypes) surrounding you. Sometimes this happens spontaneously through a traumatic or dramatic experience. Sometimes it happens through patient practice and preparation. Either way, once the unknown is glimpsed, a desire rises to find the doorway out of your present set of limitations and walk through it.

The exercises and meditations in this workbook are designed to take you through that doorway. The path begins now. The point of power is here.

WE ARE ONE COSMIC ENERGY PATTERN, the god-us in formation.

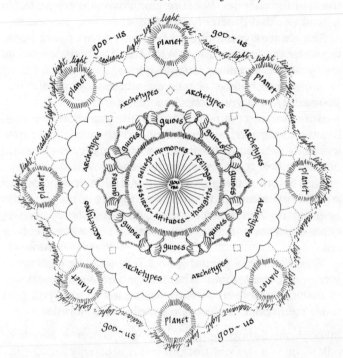

Goddess information··· god··· us··· in··· formation

Getting Ready

Preparation: A healthy physical body is the best overall preparation for any journey. Yet sometimes sickness lights the fires for change. Whatever condition you are in, begin now to see that greater health and well-being are ahead.

The choices you make each moment affect your body. Consider the food you eat. What has it experienced in its life? Was it raised and prepared in love? Did it live in a poor environment? Its love or pain are vibrations you take into yourself. How is your consciousness affected?

Bring life into yourself. Through the ingestion of whole, healthy foods and the movement and stillness of the physical body, you allow the flow of a continually creative and healing power to do its regenerative work within you.

Just before settling down for meditation, it is helpful to let the body move and make noise. Dance or do yoga, run or jump up and down, scream, moan, babble, hum or chant—anything active and noisy will release pent-up tensions and emotions. Afterwards, stillness is natural.

Then go to your sacred space. This could be a corner of your room or a temple. Wherever you go again and again to meditate, there the energy will be left to help you next time. Your space will contain your highest vibration.

Invocation: Sitting calmly, cross-legged on a bench or pillow, or in a straight-backed chair, is usually better than lying down because of the tendency to fall asleep when prone. Call the powers to your side. Invite those Spirits and Guides with whom you wish to communicate. A prayer from your heart is best.

Contemplation: Some time can be spent deciding on your focus for this particular meditation. Look over your life situation, sorting out the areas of concern. A Guide is like

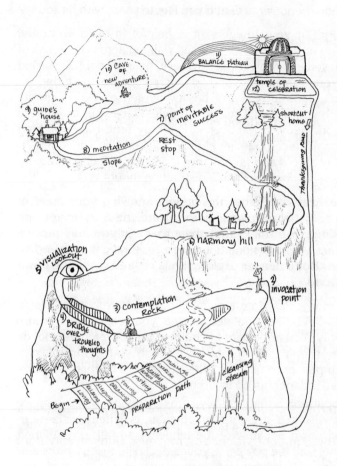

The Path

a good friend; what would you like to share with hir today?

Bridge: In your imagery, it is helpful to build an actual bridge and experience yourself walking across it. Get all of your senses involved. See it, feel it, hear the sounds around it. Your kinesthetic body (which you are in during all meditations and dreams) has its own senses. Do not simply watch yourself as if seeing a movie. Place your awareness in your body in the scene. The only time the "watching yourself" technique is valuable is when you would like to replay an old and painful memory without feeling it again. On the bridge, toss aside distracting thoughts.

Visualization: Across the bridge, knowing your point of focus, visualize a clear path toward the answer you are seeking. This may simply be a road. Or you may receive the answer at this point, in which case, give thanks and be done. But if deeper exploration is desired, continue down the road.

Harmony: Pass into a place of perfect harmony, a hillside or valley. Feel the peace, see yourself relaxing more deeply. You may want to count down, to watch the clouds carry thoughts away, to go through your body relaxing each part or to use any other method of deepening relaxation and increasing awareness.

Waterfall: At some point in the journey, you may find a waterfall, a stream, a pool, or pond. Always cleanse yourself here in your vision. You may also drink deeply from this source. The water is healing and renewing.

Success point: You may stop to rest and just take in the scene at any point along the way. No matter how far you go, allow yourself to feel successful. Never go on forcing yourself into a struggle. Sometimes a simple change of image will alleviate discomfort and distraction. Outside sounds can be incorporated into your imagery. You can create helpers along the way to give you nurturing, an angel to brush your aura, a gnome to dance with, a deer to whisper in your ear a magical spell. Be fantastic. Arouse your emotion.

Meditation: Eventually the Inner World seems to be evolving by itself. Enjoy it. Observe it. Let it happen. Don't stop to analyze it until you are finished with the entire meditation period. You *will* remember everything that happened. You can write it down or share it later.

Guide's house: Down the road, you will find the house of your Guide. Your Guide will always be a totally loving presence. Ask the Guide to allow the Light of the Great Spirit to shine through hir presence. A true Guide is always comfortable with higher energies. If you have a background of Christianity, you may find familiar faces in your journey. Your Guide may be a saint. Jesus may speak with you now and then. Or you might meet Buddha. Accept and be glad. All must eventually find comfort with the religious force of their past. Nothing happened by accident. It may be time for you to understand the deeper reasons for your upbringing in a certain religious tradition.

The Guide is your friend. Treat the Guide as you would any great friend. Present your ideas, your questions, your desires. Ask the Guide to explore the answers with you. Whenever you would like to meet an archetype of the tarot, ask the Guide to go with you. S/he is your support in all challenges. At times, even when you are not meditating, you may find the Guide at your side. The long journey I have described is not always necessary in order to make contact. Your meditation experience may begin at any point along the way. You and your Guide will decide.

New adventure: Your Guide can take you to a library where you can look up information on yourself or things that interest you. You may attend classes in certain things. You may meet archetypes and work with them. You may meet other teachers, ones who have lived famous lives on Earth and ones you have never known. You may travel around the world or to other planets. There are no boundaries here, except that you ask permission to enter the awareness of anyone you meet.

Balance: When your conversation or adventure has come to completion, ask the Guide if there is anything you need to do to assure the continuing balance in your life now that you have this new information. Always leave with an image of balance in the situation or surround it with white light and let it disappear.

Celebration: You may receive gifts along your way. Take them into your body. When you need them later, they will be there. You may also give gifts. Rejoice in all that has happened. Occasionally, your meditation will be all celebration. Sometimes the Guides plan festive events when we have achieved a certain goal toward which we were working. Always receive and appreciate. It will come naturally.

Thanksgiving: The shortcut home from your journey is the road of thanksgiving. Be thankful for everything that you have in your life that allows you to express as you do. Take your power and your talents, your insight and inspiration and put them into use in your daily life. The paradise within must be made manifest in the world without.

You will find your outer world changing as you gather experiences on the inner planes. You may think of the Inner World as a dream. But remember to think of the outer world as a dream as well. It, too, is full of guides and symbols, clues and metaphors, Gods and Goddesses. Just as an exercise, the next time you are in pain in the "real" world, tell yourself it is just a dream and wake up into the Inner World of your own creation. Change the scene, give it a different meaning, and you will find that the outer world begins to change as well. It is a delicate process, like making fine lace. You are the creator of your life pattern as you work with the light-threads of energy from the inner being. You are the weaver of worlds with the yarn of the Gods.

The Traveler's Guide

People: People you may encounter along the way and how to respond to them:

Friends: Give them appreciation for their place in your life.

Relatives: Give them what you feel they need.

World leaders: Give them the information they lack, to aid in their decision making.

Animals: Ask them to lead you to your destination. They are embodiments of instinct.

The needy: Give them healing. Wrap it as a gift to be opened when they are ready to receive it.

The struggling: Show them another way to live.

Fear, the Guardian: Talk about your options. Find out how to be prepared for what comes next in your life path.

Sexual tempters: Ask them what part of yourself you need to love, then love it. Ask them how you might align this aspect of yourself and all your desires with your highest purpose.

Monsters: Befriend them or bid them to be gone in the name of a High One. They can live only off of the energy that you are willing to give them. Take it away or transform them with your Light. State your higher purpose. Ask your Guide to assist you in reaching a higher state of consciousness. Then go on past the monsters.

Silly things: Ask them to present their deeper side. Even silly images should not be rejected. They often evolve into profound teachings. Your imagination has to draw upon the images you currently have available. It will get beyond silliness if you give it a chance.

Language: The soul thinks in images; the soul lives in images; the soul nourishes itself on images.

The images you *dwell on* tend to materialize in your life. You can image-in a reality. "If you can hold it in your mind, you can hold it in your hand." —Laurel Elizabeth Keyes

At times, you may receive your inner information through songs. Sometimes you may feel like speaking "nonsense" that will sound like another language. It may be that you just need a certain vibration to aid your process and that you might get stuck if there were content to the sounds. Accept whatever comes through. Listen. There will be plenty of time to think intellectually about the happenings after the meditation is through.

Customs: Once again, observe, accept, and appreciate the intent of whom and what you find. Dreamlike things that would be impossible in your usual outer world may happen.

This is normal and fine.

Gifts: Give and receive gracefully. Take the gifts into your body. Or find them in the outer world and keep them as objects of power. Let them remind you of your inner experience.

Currency: Love is the universal currency. Use it freely.

Sightseeing: At times, you may not be able to see your Guide or others clearly. Perhaps you will glimpse only a foot or a hand. Often this is to avoid the onslaught of preconceptions you have about certain body types or appearances. The feeling vibration is the best way to know your Guide. In time, when love is established between you and your Guide, and the bond is made, a face may be given. Never think of yourself as a failure because you are not "seeing" things. Simply do what you are able to do.

Diary: A journal of any trip is a fond remembrance. In the inner journey especially, it is often very heartening to read back through your beginning stages and see the progress you have made. It also helps you to see the desires you have brought into reality, the things you have manifested, the changes through which you have gone.

Tickets, please: This flight is free. You can go anywhere you want to go, forward in time or back through lives before. You are in complete control. Step lively, now.

A word about "making it up": The imagination has been much maligned. Its purpose has not been understood by many. You are starting the process of re-educating yourself as to its proper usage.

There is nothing, absolutely nothing, that exists in what we call the real world that has not been produced through imagination. Imagination is the source of all ideas. It is something natural and continuous, like grass growing or water running. You can tap into it at any time. With this natural gift of imagination, we take the elements of the natural world and form them into new, very real things. Imagination precedes all manifestation.

You might say, if you want a Guide, you must make one up. But this doesn't acknowledge the mysterious power that gives you this ability to make things up. It also diminishes the role of the Guide in activating and dwelling within your vision. It would be closer to the truth to say that you build a house, your body, and the Guide, the power of God, comes to live there. You are co-creators.

You did not invent imagination. Without it, your life is dull and perhaps impossible. It is a gift to you, but you alone can use the gift. Your role is all important.

It is only by your respect for your imagination and your developing it by proper usage, as you would any muscle in your body or your intellect, that you can share in the magical world it can provide for you.

Do not be afraid to "make things up." Without your conscious knowledge, you are making up the entire world you already live in. Indeed, others are helping you to create it, perhaps even taking more power in its creation than you are. You allow this. Thus, you can be ruled by the imaginations of others or you can begin to accept responsibility for imagining a better world and thereby beginning its possibility for creation.

Use your imagination fully to reach what I call the higher realms. All this means is to go for the very best you can dream. From there, God will take over. Seeing how willing you are to use this powerful tool and do your part, the Great Spirit of all life will begin to offer you things beyond your imagining. You will hit points in your meditative journeys where some greater power will take over and provide information beyond your knowing and wisdom beyond your capacity. You will have tapped the sources of inspiration and creativity, the well of wholeness and holiness that lies waiting, still, inside you.

1 RESOURCES

Number and Meaning: 1, I am.

Traditional Name: The Magician

Medicine Woman Energy: The Resourceful One Using the Tools at Hand

Affirmation: "I am a resource of the eternally creating and sustaining Spirit of Life. All that I need to carry out the divine plan is before me."

The Card Speaks: "I am the Medicine Wo/man. Through my choice of actions, I bring life to my people. Creator who lives within me has given me stewardship of that which I see before me. My tools are the Stones, the Earth substance of which all things are made; the Pipes, symbol of all channels of creative energy, including the body in which I dwell; the Arrows, showing me the power of clear, one-pointed mind; and Bowls, allowing me to offer my love and receive the blessings of those who come to share their gifts with me.

"I refuse to give my attention to things that limit me or deny my wholeness. To all life I am connected. I understand the sexual flow within me to be the fuel of creation that can be channelled for those purposes I hold within my heart. I value this life force and direct it toward right relationship with all beings.

"I let go of those things I no longer value, keeping that

31

which I love and for which I can care. These things then bring me comfort, support and help according to their purpose. I possess only by nature of my caring. With my wealth, I support the things I believe in, the things that enhance life on my planet. I withdraw this support from those things and institutions that bring harm to living beings. All things are tools. All tools are as magic wands that can create the world of my highest vision. I accept the powers within me. I am content with the tools that are before me. Within the Great Plan of Creation I trust that I am given what I can best use. My talent and inspiration combine with the material world around me in keeping with the ultimate balance of all that is."

Self-questioning: Where do I spend my money? Are these the places I want to support? Do I give the gift of my sexual expression to the one I would like to become? You become that on which you dwell. Your money is energy supporting the world you choose. Sex and money are powerful energies you will more thoroughly understand as you read the chapters on the "Four Powers."

Auras, the energy fields surrounding human bodies, begin to blend at deeper and deeper levels in a sexual encounter. Your destiny and that of your partner begin to combine. Are you giving this intimate gift to one you admire enough to become so entwined? Do you wish to accept this person's wholeness, to carry his/her pack on your back? Is your load lighter by the sharing?

Exercise: Begin to arrange your living quarters in the way that gives you power, getting rid of what you never use, allowing these things to fulfill their purpose of usefulness with someone else, and blessing the things that bring you satisfaction by your caring for them. Your home is your personal world of resources. It is your first-level manifestation of power. Make sure it supports your true being.

Meditation: Imagine yourself as a Medicine Woman. See before you the four symbols of power, your tools in the manifest world: a stone, a pipe, an arrow, a bowl. Lift them one at a time and ask them to speak to you about yourself.

Visualization: See yourself using one of your tools in a new way, perhaps in a way in which you formerly felt yourself incapable. Feel the power of expressing in this new way. See others noticing and complimenting you on this new capability.

Remember, your stone may be any Earth object; your pipe something that is a hollow channel of energy such as a flute or your body; your arrow can be any focused thought; your bowl is any container of your love and devotion.

Astrological Sign: Mercury

Colors: Bright yellow for mental concentration and alertness. Rose for feelings of universal love. Pale violet or silver gray, like the smoke from the sacred pipe, for spiritual upliftment. Rich reds and oranges for the clay of Earth to remind you of her beauty.

The Mysteries

The Magician, The Resourceful One Using the Tools at Hand, introduces us to the mysteries. The tarot is divided into two groups of understandings: the Major Arcana or Great Mystery and the Minor Arcana or Lesser Mysteries. The Major Arcana are the prime spiritual forces in your life. The Minor Arcana are the four forces you must reckon with in your day-to-day life.

The Minor Arcana I call the Four Powers. You will learn

more about them as we enter that section of this book. They are represented by the suits of Stones, Pipes, Arrows, and Bowls. The Resourceful One knows that these forces are powers innate to every human being. They constantly confront us as challenges and we deal with them by activating from within their corresponding powers.

The Major Arcana or Great Mystery begin in us as a basic life force, the desire to live. The life force blossoms into sexual energy and travels throughout our lives as creative expression. Eventually this force takes us higher and higher and becomes identifiable as the spiritual force. The cards of the Great Mystery (Major Arcana) show how this force carries us through life to our final enlightenment. The cards can also be read in relation to any one process in which we may be involved. In other words, they speak macrocosmically of the "Big Picture" and microcosmically of each little event through which we must pass.

Our bodies contain seven primary spiritual energy centers. These are called chakras. Though different religious systems assign different colors to each chakra, many agree on the following arrangement.

Violet	Top of the head (crown)
Indigo	Center of forehead (third eye)
Blue	Throat
Green	Heart
Yellow	Stomach area (solar plexus)
Orange	Upper pelvic area (pancreas)
Red	Base of the spine (sexual organs)

Each chakra relates to a level of consciousness. We pass

through these levels of consciousness on our way to spiritual fulfillment. The level of consciousness where you spend most of your time depends on your spiritual development. It is possible to have peak experiences only because we do not always "hang out" at the peak. It is also possible to fall below one's usual state of consciousness, for example, when you meant to act out of your heart center and ended up responding from your power center (yellow chakra).

It is not necessarily wrong to operate from a lower center at any given moment. Each center or chakra has important experiences to offer us. Each center focuses our attention in a particular way. In general, the chakra centers of consciousness provide us with desires and motivation for certain kinds of experiences that will promote some aspect of our spiritual unfolding.

Chakra	Type of Focus
Violet	Seeing life from a cosmic perspective, visionary, mystical
Indigo	Intuitive, psychic, seeing
Blue	Philosophical, speaking out, creative, conceptual
Green	Healing, honoring nature and all life forms, beginnings of unconditional love
Yellow	Intellectual, personal empowerment, recognition of one's own worth
Orange	Social, kinship ties, service to others, here and now conditions, health
Red	Survival, basic necessities, continuation of the species, ongoingness of life

At each level, sexual expression is occurring, but the experience of sexuality is different depending on the center from which you are operating.

Crown/Violet: You see your partner as God and your sexuality as an expression of your devotion to the One

Third eye/Indigo: You have the ability to relate to your partner's High Self. You are attracted by your vision of the other's aura or innermost being. You also want your true Self to be recognized.

Throat/Blue: You are attracted by creative expressions, sound of voice, sensual music, lighting, aesthetics. You also want to be heard at a very deep and sincere level of your being.

Heart/Green: You are attracted by constancy of love, ability to work through trouble spots, kindness, fairness, compassion. You very much desire romantic happiness because this is the first level at which you can see the possibility for eternal love, though it is here that your most difficult lessons about how to achieve it are learned.

Solar plexus/Yellow: You are attracted by another's intellect or personal power. There is a feeling of admiration or awe. At the same time, you have a need to exercise your own power and realize your own qualities. Power plays and ego trips could be rampant here, but you could also respectfully bring out each other's unique powers. It is easy to be jealous or competitive here, but life will provide you with experiences so that you can get beyond these emotions.

Pelvic/Orange: You are attracted by emotional kinship, ease of relationship, affection, and social compatibility. You enjoy taking care of each other in a variety of ways.

Family is a main focus.

Base of spine/Red: You are attracted by the basic polarity between self and other. You are acting instinctually out of the body's basic drive to propagate the species, to reproduce the "self." This is your basic fire of desire, yet the flame must rise as your spiritual consciousness rises.

Each level of sexuality has its supreme value. None of them is negative in itself. Yet a person may become involved in negativity, self-doubt, or fear anywhere along the way. The tendency is, of course, lesser at higher levels, but at these levels the desire to reach perfection can be a very hard taskmaster.

So, appreciate where you are. Enjoy it fully. Learn what you can. All experiences will be yours in time. The great mystery will provide every experience you need in order to move you along the path to spiritual and sexual fulfillment. As stated previously, sexuality, creativity, and spirituality are all outflowerings of each other. The energy of life moves through your body and your consciousness, attracting you to the people and situations that will eventually bring out the best in you. Appreciate what each opportunity brings. Live each moment to the best of your ability. Thus does your ability grow.

Tarot Path through the Mystery

The cards of the Major Arcana can be lined up, three abreast, with the chakra centers of consciousness. Each set of three cards relates to a specific color and center of expression. As you look at this alignment, you can see that it applies to the total picture of your life in general and also to the experience of your relationships along the way.

First, you are given three basics with which to start life

or any process within your life. In order to begin a relationship, whether with a person, place, thing, or with life itself,
you must have the following.

Survival basics: Red level/Root chakra

0 Seed: The Seed idea. The willingness of the Fool to
   step out into the unknown.

1 Resources: Whatever it takes is there before you;
   you need only to recognize it and utilize it.

2 Seeker: The path to further knowledge begins with
   your own self. All you need to do is trust and act intuitively.

Kinship bonds: Orange level/Pelvic chakra

3 Bounty: You have been given your basic body, intellect, family, and a level of wealth and place of living
   with which to begin your Earth journey. See and appreciate what you already have. Take advantage of
   the gifts before you.

4 Command: There are talents and abilities within you
   that are more than enough to tackle the situation at
   hand. Go for it.

5 Peacemaker: Here you must interface with the world,
   showing your stuff. It is here that you learn what is of
   benefit to that world, and what the world wants and
   will accept from you.

Personal power: Yellow level/Solar plexus chakra

6 Ecstasy: Your inner gifts have met with outer expression. Your Self has been released.

7 Warrior: The world has recognized you in some way.

Achievement is realized. You are encouraged to go on.

8 Healing: The life force that flows through you now becomes a beneficial energy to self and others.

Harmony: Green level/Heart chakra

9 Guide: Here you meet your higher portion, the Guide or High Self, who begins to help you through any obstacles and to spur you to further growth.

10 Harvest: Rewards come in for all that you have done thus far. It is time for respite and review.

11 Balance: You see that there is a larger balance to keep than merely your own. You grow in humility and ability.

Creative: Blue level/Throat chakra

12 Vision: You are given a vision of the world as it could be. A role in that unfolding is laid before you.

13 Sunset: What has led to now is passing away. It is no longer possible to be who you were. You have seen a greater Self, a distant reality yet to be manifest. The call leads you through the death of the past and on to new life.

14 Blend: You begin to integrate past and future in a creative and visionary blend.

Imagination: Indigo level/Third eye chakra

15 Trickster: You begin to experience the snares of the world. Yet you also begin to know that all the cultural world is created by human mind and action utilizing divine energy. Your imagination allows you to

envision other possibilities. You travel between feelings of hopelessness and wonder, gloomy doom and utopian excitement.

16 Pierced Shield: Everything seems to come apart around you. Yet it is merely the thought structure that kept you limited that is breaking away. You, in a higher version, are being released.

17 The Grandfathers: You seek and receive guidance from those who have traveled this path before.

Renewal: Violet level/Crown chakra

18 The Grandmothers: You relax into the arms of the Great Mother, the nurturing energy of the realization that you are not alone. There are many caretakers of Earth and all her beings.

19 Rebirth: You begin to see how something even greater might occur, and you begin to look at your particular life as but a small, yet necessary part of some huge all-encompassing plan that has taken everything into account. You feel as free as a child again, in a wonder-filled world cared for by a divine family.

20 Discernment: Now you begin to act with higher judgment. You have confidence in your decision-making, for you have been shown both your importance and your insignificance. You see that you are a stitch in the cloth of time, but perhaps the one that saves nine.

Bliss: White level/Merges with the eternal

21 Dancer: You are on top of the world. Not caught in the drama of life, you participate freely. Transcen-

dence of all struggle. The joy of being here now is yours.

In terms of sexuality, the Seed is your attractive power. There is a force within you that attracts. The Fool, Seed, within you also attracts you to others. You are drawn to those people, things and situations that have information you need in order to advance on your spiritual journey. Everyone, everything, you are attracted to has the potential of bringing out some creative aspect of your being. The people and things you come into relationship with challenge or entice your inner being out into manifestation. Thus, every relationship reveals you to yourself and brings your talents to the world.

You may have felt **Fool**ish at times when you wanted to attract someone to yourself. You had to take a risk, to put yourself out, to step off the cliff, to toss the seeds of Self to the winds of fate. As the Fool, you took steps toward that which was attracting you. It may not have turned out to be what you thought it would be, but it came to you in a form sufficiently attractive to entice you forward into the lessons you needed to learn. You were "Fooled" into your own growing.

The Fool in you keeps the life force flowing. The Fool flirts with possibilities, and before you know it, you are in so far that you have to utilize all of your powers to realize that potential you initially imagined. The Fool holds out a hope and a promise and does hir best to make the trip enjoyable. The Fool fills life with fun and desire. The Fool opens doors and lets you fall . . . right into the situations that will bring about your perfection. Fools fall in love, and in love, everything is possible.

The Magician's power is to realize that you have what it takes to attract everyone and everything you need. You have the tools at hand both to get love and to keep love happening. Sexually speaking, you have all the basic equipment right within your body and in your environment in order to make your fondest dreams come true. The power of life and creation flows through *this body* in the ways that *you command* through your thoughts and images. Your major tool in life is this sexual creative force . . . your major lessons—all twenty-two of them—consist of learning how to use it.

You also have four minor sets of tools or ways to meet your earth-plane needs. The Magician, Resourceful One Using the Tools at Hand, is the master craftsman when it comes to these earthly tools. The earth, air, fire, and water are the elements s/he uses. These elements are combined in the four suits of the Minor Arcana: Stones, Pipes, Arrows, and Bowls. They are the medicine bag of the Medicine Woman. She magically arranges her life to suit her needs with the very same elements that puzzle and overwhelm others.

With the life-force creative/sexual/spiritual energy that she embodies, she arranges her personal world or resources in a way that gives expression to her loftiest goals and most deeply held convictions. As you continue through the lessons to come, you will see how she, the Medicine Woman inside you, continues to enhance not only her sexual energy, but her creative abilities, and her spiritual qualities as well.

Take stock of your resources. Accentuate the positive. And move on to the lesson of the Seeker.

2 SEEKER

Number and Meaning: 2, Self-reflection

Traditional Name: The High Priestess

Medicine Woman Energy: Seeker of the Light Within

Affirmation: "My world is a reflection of my relationship to all that is. Through my image and word, Great Spirit's wisdom takes form."

The Card Speaks: "I am the Seeker, High Priestess of my own destiny. I look first within myself for the cause of all that I see before me. My world is but a manifestation of that which is taking place within my psyche. My soul speaks to me in images, telling me of possibility. I hold in my own mind a book of knowledge of all past events and those to come. I have access to the Universal Memory through my ever-deepening states of meditation and attunement. I am the questioner of all that is, lifting the veils that cloud my inner knowing.

"I am the virgin, containing the unfertilized seeds of my potential creations. I have learned to say no to that which does not benefit myself and to say yes to the interactions and situations that nourish me. I am a child of the moon, studying my cycles, my moods, my phases. I learn from my body, which speaks to me through its feelings and responses. I observe my patterns and changes. The mirror of myself reflects the Goddess."

Self-questioning: Describe your life in seven-year cycles. What patterns do you see? Make a list of each year of your life, starting with the year of your birth and going up to the present year. List one significant event after each year. What do you see?

Exercise: Keep track of your cycles and the phases of the moon. Do you see a relationship?

Meditation: One by one, send your awareness through each part of your body, giving the command to relax and heightening your perception of that which is going on within yourself. Think of each part of your body as a room in a great library containing books with all the answers to your questions. Every cell is another volume of information. Pause anywhere and visualize yourself picking up one of these books. Begin reading.

Visualization: See yourself *having already accomplished* something you have been wanting to do. Focus on the qualities that have come about within yourself in order to have made this accomplishment. Notice what you are wearing in this new role. Who is around you? How do they feel about your success? Who comes to compliment and support you? Whom have you benefited? After you feel complete with this visioning process—fifteen minutes will usually do—go out into the world and *do something* this new you would do.

Do a second visualization in the same manner. This time ask yourself: How do you feel? Where are you? How did you get there? What obstacles did you overcome? What inner resources did you use to get where you are? Again, when complete, go out into the world and act in confidence.

Astrological Sign: The moon

Colors: Moon-blue and the silky, sensuous deeper blues that invite you inward to explore.

The Reflecting Body

Your body holds knowledge of all lives you have ever lived. It is filled with experience. The computer and its micromemory system has nothing over the amazing human body and its storehouse of information. The Seeker asks you to explore your body, to learn from it, to know its secrets. Once again, your own sexual nature entices you to discover the physical self. Discovery of the physical self brings awareness of other levels of your being. Soon you are asking, "From where does true ecstasy come?" And the Fool, that brave adventurer inside you, leads you further down the path.

Just as the Magician, Resourceful One, has observed the primal energy ever-present within and has seen the creations that have been made with it, the Seeker looks beyond. The Seeker is not satisfied with mere outer appearance, but wants to know why, what makes it so. The Magician wields energy skillfully, but the Seeker wants to understand how the energy came to be passing through in this way and what else it can do. One of the discoveries the Seeker makes is that food affects her vibration, both her sense of well-being and her energy level. It affects her mood, her strength, her ability to search, for search takes concentration and endurance. Looking in the mirror of Self requires clear mind and body.

You cannot go inside and expect to find a peaceful place to study with a gurgling stomach, an aching back, a stopped-up nose, and weary muscles. You must become a High Priestess who takes the nutritional elements in a combination that cleans and builds the temple of her indwelling God-self. The Seeker seeks health not only to feel good day by day, but to allow her the peace in which to explore her higher nature unobstructed.

Bodies try to heal themselves. This is their basic nature. For the most part, if you have not severely abused your body, time and patience will allow proper healing to take place. On the other hand, the world we live in is filled with stresses and temptations to ignore the body's wisdom. Often our strongly empowered intellects, the rational side of our beings, overrule the body's suggestions. The body begins to accumulate the recovery periods you have denied it. It must, therefore, become sicker and sicker until you will allow it to have the series of short recovery periods you have denied it. This results in an illness that requires a long layoff.

Your body attempts each season to bring itself back into the harmony of nature around it. In the spring, it wants to be active; in the summer, to work and rest intermittently; in the fall, to harvest and take stock of itself; in the winter, to sit back, reflect and prepare for another new time to come. When the seasonal weather changes, your body will often try to cleanse itself in preparation for the changing environment in which it must live. You can assist it by fasting or eating a particular diet suitable for the time of year.

Heading toward warm weather, your body desires fresh fruits, lighter foods, alive, raw, newly sprouted foods. Wild foods, the first to grow in the spring, are particularly cleansing, a tonic to the system. When the garden is in full leaf, fresh greens and root vegetables are in order. In the fall, the hardier squashes, potatoes, and heavier vegetables call to you. Grains are harvested and stored for winter consumption, when the body is happy to have a bowl of hot rice or some fresh whole wheat bread. Though we live in a culture and time period when we can eat foods out of season, it is not necessarily healthy to do so.

If you have ignored your body's suggestions and have

eaten sugar, white bread, red meat, rich foods, chemically treated foods, or covered up your body's responses with medical or nonmedical drugs, alcohol, or cigarettes for more than twenty years, you should realize that you are in serious trouble. Even if you have misindulged for only ten years, your body will have a few healing crises to undergo before it will begin to respond gently to natural changes of season and cycle.

A healing crisis is an event that seems like an illness, by all outward appearances, but is something triggered by an act of health. An act of health is any action that you take which is naturally and nutritionally sound. Examples of acts of health that might trigger a healing crisis are as diverse as the following: fasting, eating only fresh, whole foods for a week, refraining from coffee, cigarettes, drugs, or chemically treated foods for a few days, meeting an exceptionally high spiritual person, feeling someone's unconditional love for you, getting a massage, walking in a beautiful natural wilderness, viewing a poignant scene, or even getting space and time to be alone when you haven't had solitude for a long time.

What you must understand is that no matter how uncomfortable the healing crisis is, the disease that would occur if you do not allow the healing to take place is twice as distressing. If you sense your body to have stored toxins from past abuses, go easy on yourself. Take steps slowly and gently to improve your health. Begin listening and paying attention to what your body asks you to do.

There are many fine healing programs available. There are hundreds of books on natural health and physical vitality. Your local health food store or holistic health practitioner is the best place to begin to look for the knowledge you need. But inside yourself is the real doctor. S/he may be currently incapacitated by your ignorance, but feed hir knowledge and s/he will come alive. If you currently have a severe illness, read as many books as you can get your hands on about case histories of people who have cured themselves through visualization, herbs, and fresh foods and juices or fasting. Testimonials are numerous and very inspiring.

Meanwhile, substitute any health food or practice for any death food or practice in which you are currently engaged. Spend a quiet moment with your body, and your body will quickly tell you which is which. When you have one success, go for the next.

3 BOUNTY

Number and Meaning: 3, Expression, fertility

Traditional Name: The Empress

Medicine Woman Energy: Bountiful Earth Mother

Affirmation: "I am a fertile ground of possibility. My talents, abilities, and experiences now combine and compel me toward my highest expression. As I allow myself to be nurtured, I am confident that I will flower."

The Card Speaks: "Some have called me Mother Nature, others the Goddess of Earth. By any name, I am a woman in a paradise of creation. I am the lush beauty of the natural world. I am pregnant with potential. I control the material world through the images I hold in my mind and give them fuel through my love. I recognize the laws of nature and work *with* them. This is my power. My mind draws from what I observe and integrates this with what can be. My world is therefore in balance.

I live in the garden of my delights. I choose my concepts wisely, like the flowers I choose to plant. Every idea is a seed. I water what is beautiful. I am the womb of creation, through which the fullness of life flows into every thought I dwell upon, giving it life. I bear the children who are the parts of myself needing to be expressed. As the Cosmic Mother, I have given you life in order that you may blossom into your fullness.

"I preserve my youthful vitality by my sensuous participation in life. With the plant ones, I speak, asking them to give to me their nourishment. With all things and creatures, I am in constant telepathic communication, guiding their energies in my life. There is no thought that is not heard, never is a word unheeded. Thus I have abandoned worry, for it calls that which I do not want. My call is the medicine call for all that is beauty into my life."

Self-questioning: Think of your mind as a garden. What is growing there?

Exercise: Walk in nature. Begin to talk with the beings there. Then stop to listen for the telepathic answers.

Meditation: Go now into a relaxed state. It would be beneficial if you are able to be outdoors or to hear the outdoors. Walk into the garden (mentally) of the Earth Mother. Ask her to tell you of your hidden potential, your talent not yet used, the child living within you as unexpressed Self. Ask her what your next step might be to bring forth this new being.

Visualization: Imagine yourself as the Great Mother. Feel yourself sitting in the midst of a lush landscape, surrounded by radiant colors and bright sounds. Listen. See. Make everything very clear. Notice details. Notice textures. And *feel.* And intensify those feelings. Stay as long as you like. Be nourished.

Astrological Sign: Venus

Foods and colors: Emerald green is the color of Bounty, nature's backdrop to all the riches of Earth. Go outside and enjoy a forest or surround yourself with living plants. In early spring, you may want to forage for wild foods. There are plenty of books on the subject at your local library. This is a sure way to begin to realize that Earth Mother is always trying to provide for us.

Wear her rich greens. Green is the color of balance and of plenty. It is the security of all that grows by itself.

Turning the Past into Pleasure

Many people have difficulty thinking of their past as something positive and appreciating the experiences that brought them to their present state of being. It is true that many people have endured real hardship and trauma in their lives, yet continuing to dwell on these past problems seldom does anything but handicap the person in the present.

One of the lessons of the Bounty card is to appreciate all that has come before, to realize that, at worst, it was all compost for what is growing inside you now. You can turn painful memories into a rich soil in which to develop the garden of your present delights. You will need a partner willing to work with you on this experiment, perhaps someone who also wants to transform one of their own past memories. Then, bring to mind the event that you feel most often trips you up time and again, something you wish had not happened quite the way it did. When it is clear in your mind—only one at a time, please—continue with your friend in the following way.

1. Tell the event as a sad story.

2. Tell the event from another person's point of view.

3. Tell the event from the perspective of an imagined High Being.

4. Tell the event as if it were a very happy occurrence.

5. Tell the event as if it were a situation comedy.

Your friend only listens to each telling, perhaps asking questions for clarification and to encourage a full retelling of the tale each time. Then tell the story a sixth time, this time in a way that feels empowering to you. It may be a combination of some of the other ways you told it or it may be totally new. Then, ask your partner which way s/he liked the story best and why.

Now, go into your relaxed state and re-vision the entire event just the way you would have liked it to be. This is your new memory. It is now a creation that will bring forth bounty.

You may at first feel that this new memory is not "true." But if you interviewed everyone who was originally involved in the event as you first recalled it, each person would have a different version of the "truth." The real truth is whatever will set you free of the limitation this "memory" has put on you. You are taking power over the past by re-membering. You are perceiving the situation differently, just as each person initially involved perceives it differently than you ever did. Every past experience can be a gift if you work with it this way.

Your life is rich in memories that guide your present. Rearrange them to totally support the you that you are becoming now.

4 COMMAND

Number and Meaning: 4, Form, order

Traditional Name: The Emperor

Medicine Woman Energy: Taking Command for the Good of All

Affirmation: "I now create the structures through which all of my gifts will be actualized. I am the governor of my world. I am the ruler of my life. From Limitless Spirit, I draw all things needed for right action."

The Card Speaks: "I am the Emperor/Chief, creator of the overall structure that takes into account the many abilities, talents and experiences you have discovered within and relates them to the world's needs. Through the Empress/Bounty in yourself, you learned of these gifts in your being. Now, through me, you will learn how to give them physical form.

"You have journeyed as the Fool/Seed, willing to take a risk to move forward. Then, as a Magician/Resourceful One, you saw the tools you have to use along the way. As the High Priestess/Seeker, you realized your responsibility for that which you experience. At the same time, along the way, you discovered an abundance of good ideas, high goals, and personal ambitions. You experienced the bountiful feeling of the Empress when you saw the abilities, talents, and knowledge that have been planted in your consciousness. Now it is time to find a structure that can allow this whole Self to come through in fullness.

"Your thoughts and images dictate your reality. You must take command now. It is time to make decisions that benefit your whole being and that of the Earth, your dwelling place. I tell you, you are the maker of your personal law. The definitions of the meaning of your experiences constitute (make into law) suggestions that are accepted, without reservation, by your consciousness. You define what you see, many times without thinking. Realize, you have choice in your definition, in your response, to any situation. This is your point of power."

Self-questioning: Are you in the work situation you desire? Are you in the relationship you want?

Exercise: Take a subject you experience difficulty with, then write a list of one-sentence beliefs you hold about that subject. Concerning money, for example, your list should look something like this:

"I think rich people are. . . . "
"I never have enough. . . . "
"Times are rough because. . . . "
"I can't get. . . . "
"My parents wouldn't. . . . "
"I wish I could. . . . "

Then read over your list. These sentences are the laws of your life in this area. Can you think of better ones? Use these "better ones" as your affirmations. It is helpful to make signs or cards and to put them in places where you will unconsciously notice them many times throughout the day. Remember, you are being programmed by all you see and hear. Television, radio, magazines, movies are all subtle commands to your subconscious. You may want to replace some of these suggestions with your own. Choose your self-programming consciously. Be the commander of your own reality.

Meditation: In your inner awareness, go to the tepee of the Chief. Place your doubts and fears in the central fire. Give the Chief permission to speak to you, to reach through any barriers that you may unconsciously put up, and to give you insight as to your true place in the world. The Chief may call other Medicine People into the circle. A pipe may be passed. Inhale the Light of the Spirit that you may be able to see clearly your own path.

Visualization: Image-in the picture of yourself as a very prosperous and powerful leader. Now step into that image and feel the qualities you would carry into the role. See that you can be kind, generous; that you can plan, administrate, guide; that you can be a peacemaker, a diplomat, an emissary, a counselor. Your words guide others. Your thoughts and ideas affect them. Rules you make are carried out, and visions you have are manifest in the material world. You are impeccably prosperous.

Astrological Sign: Aries

Colors: Scarlet to excite action. Purple for the royal feelings of rulership. You may wish to experiment with the precious stones or feathers or other talismans to find what brings you feelings of strength.

Flowing with the Go

Command is not power over the force, but working with the force. It is the taking advantage of a flow already strongly going. Consider these forces and whether you currently have command of them: money, sex, time, and energy.

The Chief must consider how to utilize not only hir own, but each individual's talents to take advantage of the tribe's innate wealth. Your tribe may be your family, peer group, business staff, or spiritual circle. As leader, you must be wise enough to recognize the true inclinations and abilities within each person. Then you must figure out how to encourage the full expression of these innate qualities in a way that benefits the whole. These innate tendencies will always be the things that make the individual feel fulfilled and happy during the process. What is "good for" the individual is good for the whole. No one is asked to give up the Self to sacrifice for the tribe.

Likewise, the Chief looks at the larger forces of life, not only the forces of nature, but the forces of society, and does hir best to work with the flow of these forces. Once again, a utilization of the energy-in-process is called for. It is not a giving up or giving in, but a taking advantage of. It is using the momentum of what is already happening. If the fish swim upstream, you go there to catch them; you don't give up eating. You harness the wind with windmills and generate power for your own needs; you don't sit around wishing for electricity. The flowing river turns the water wheel, runs the mill, grinds the grain. Rain falling from the roof fills the barrel for watering your garden.

In modern life, the amount of money you have is a power, however inadequate you may think it to be. It is a force given to you to see if you can make wise choices, to see if you can maximize its potential to create the good of your choice. Of itself, it is like a lump of clay. Do you say, "This is just dirt," and throw it away, or do you become a sculptor?

It is the same with the time you have been given—your life time. How do you use it? Does every moment count? When free, do you allow the true Self to come out? Do you love, create, enjoy your time? Or is it all given to the suppression of Self to another's will? Taking command is using your will, thereby increasing your willpower.

Your thoughts are another tremendous creating force.

How do you use them? They form your world on the inner plane, setting up the patterns that manifest in the outer world. Take command.

Within every situation, there are forces at work, powers already in action. The wise Chief finds a way to use them for greater good. It is the Chief's goal always to bring better fortune to hir people and thus the Self as well. The ancient martial arts are supreme examples of learning to use the energy at hand in a physical way. The aikido master takes advantage of the direction of the opponent. Go with the direction of the fall. That which opposes you is rendered helpless to harm you.

A loss is always a new freedom as well. A gain is a steppingstone. The challenge you are given by a life situation is an opportunity to perfect a skill or quality that you will be happy to have later, as the Great Plan of the unfolding universe is put before you. You are a warrior in training. Never complain about an opportunity to hone your skills. Go forward with the fullness of your being. Take command. The non-Chief complains. The Chief sees opportunity and takes charge of the forces by setting hirself in a position that will receive the forces' benefit and diminish the likelihood of harm. You, like the Chief, have your own goals and deeply held values. These should not be set aside. The lesson of taking command is simply that you must use your mind and will to place yourself, container of these goals and values, in a position where they will be strengthened and enhanced. Go now, look at your deepest needs and desires. In what already-happening flow of energy can you place them? Stop embracing struggle. Take command.

5 PEACEMAKER

Number and Meaning: 5, Mediation

Traditional Name: The Hierophant

Medicine Woman: The Peacemaker Interfacing with the World

Affirmation: "I am the mediator between my God-self and my world. I bring the within outward, recognizing that my presentation and the world's response are just. I am at peace with all outcomes."

The Card Speaks: "I am the guiding voice speaking to you from within your heart, combining the soul's needs with those of the world. I tell you when to speak and when to be silent. I am the go-between, the bridge. I am the one who knows the ways of the world, and yet am not overwhelmed by them. I tell you how to bring your highest vision into creation. If you have listened to the tarot cards before me, you have seen what can be, you have created a supportive structure for your ideas and ideals; now, I tell you how to present yourself through these structures. I am your interface with the world.

"If you are not within a structure—be it job, relationship, or society—which supports your wholeness, you may find me suggesting 'outrageous' things. Depending on how non-beneficial your structure is for your self-actualization, I will 'cause trouble.' It is my role, in whatever way I must, to move you through the changes required for your spiritual growth. Your choice is to create a path of your choosing, or I will open the Earth before you.

"I am a master of protocol, the right ritual of every

situation. I understand completely what is expected, in conventional terms, and yet I never miss an opportunity to shine a light through any crack I see.

"At times, I have appeared as the gypsy prince holding the mysteries in my consciousness and acting intuitively in the world. I have been called the Peacemaker, for I understand every side of every dispute and always bring the polarities into balance. I realize that a suffering person suffers because she has become ready for a new and higher level of being. If you listen, I speak the way. I am the Book of Changes. I am the darkness and the dawn. I am the movement in the dance of life. Look to me for revelation of all things sacred. These are the Unchanging within the changed.

"You will hear me call you on to better things. As you pass each chance for change, you will know if you have taken the right step. You will know, for you will feel the presence of the Peacemaker inside yourself. I am with you."

Self-questioning: Am I willing to move ahead in the direction I see as best for myself or do I wait until circumstances force me to grow?

Exercise: Keep a journal this week of the guiding voice that speaks while you are out in the world in action. Jot down what the voice tells you to do, and what you actually do.

Meditation: Go for a ride in the gypsy wagon with the prince. Let him tell you how he reveals the Great Mystery to the world while only passing through. From where comes the trust that he will always be taken care of? What is his power to attract? His ability to let go? Who is this elusive stranger in yourself?

Visualization: Realize yourself as a Peacemaker. Go now, in the eye of your mind, and speak clearly where the speaking is needed. Touch where you have previously been afraid to touch. Stand up where before you have sat back in silence. Let love come through where anger lived. Feel the physical changes.

Astrological Sign: Taurus

Foods: It's time for a change. Arrange an occasion where you must eat that which you are not accustomed to eating. Break an old pattern. Learn to enjoy whatever is put before you. Notice the effect (both of the attitude and of the food) on your consciousness.

Colors: A red-orange for energy and movement. Be bright and clear. Notice others' response to you on days when you are dressing more flamboyantly and on days when you blend into the woodwork. Each can be appropriate at some times.

Peacemaking

It is wonderful to have ideas. Fantasies and high ideals inspire us and give us hope. They are seeds of future health and wealth. Yet, it is easy to let a sprouting garden of ideas die. The Seed energy must be nurtured, with the tools at hand, by you, the Resourceful One, and watered by your consciousness of self-responsibility (Seeker of the Light) and rich inner resources (Bounty) to the point of flowering.

Here you take Command, distributing the harvest to where it will do the most good. You take your best and offer it to the world, Peacemaking. You make true peace by offering your real Self in a way the world can accept. There is something in you that the world, at least some portion of the world, is waiting for.

A common problem people face is that they either believe their gifts will be rejected and so do not offer them, or they offer their gifts to people who are not interested. In the business world, it is of the utmost importance to find your niche. It is no different in other situations. If you want a successful outcome, you must not only have a good idea, but you must present it in a way that will be acceptable to a specific group of people. Many people fail because they are not acting much different from the salesman trying to sell refrigerators to Eskimos.

Often, people want to make peace with their parents. So they badger their parents to accept them, a technique that seldom works. Instead, without sacrificing their true being, they could simply "repackage themselves" by presenting their ideas in terms their parents already understand, or they could just share more fully the parts of themselves that their parents already accept. Go with the flow. If your mother likes your home cooking, share that with her instead of your enjoyment of occult books. Let go of your need to conflict with her.

Peacemaking is a fine art. It is often the art of keeping silence, letting go of the ego need to be one-up. No one was ever reformed permanently by bullying. The Peacemaker is ever watchful, however, for just the right opening to speak just enough to gain interest and respect. This way, there is no need to argue and no need to back down from your true stance. You proceed systematically and intuitively forward at a steady pace, counting every tiny advance as a success. Thus, there is no war; there is slowly expanding cooperation.

6 ECSTASY

Number and Meaning: 6, Beauty, equilibrium

Traditional Name: Lovers

Medicine Woman Energy: The Lovers, Finding the Spirit within, Unite With Ecstasy

Affirmation: "With love, I entice the inner person into relationship with the outer world. I attract what I wish to become and I radiate what I am. Beauty surrounds me. The Earth and I are one."

The Card Speaks: "We are the lovers, both within and outside of yourself. We are two parts of you. The beauty you see in the person you love is but a mirror of that beauty within yourself. As you love another, you begin to love yourself. Within you, a perfect Self dwells and begins to have expression, through love, becoming confident enough to walk out into the world. I, the Woman Attuned to Spirit, am given form through the Male Attuned to the Needs of the World. I, the Male Attuned to the Needs of the World, am given inspiration and guidance through the Woman Attuned to Spirit. The superconsciousness is manifest through the flesh in our perfect union. The word is made flesh between us. As womanness and manness are in balance, we dwell in harmony. As inspiration and guidance from within are balanced by attending to the needs of the world, we find equilibrium. It is thus in you, and in your relationships.

"We are the conscious and the subconscious, the rational and the intuitive, the work and the play, the sensitive and the sensuous. When you have reached us, you will no

61

longer see the outer world as a force against yourself. You will have brought goodness from it, and it will have brought goodness forth from you. Now the sexual energy reaches from the sensual to the super-senses. The 'kundalini' has risen. The sleeping serpent has awakened. Love now encompasses both the physical attraction on the human level and the craving for the divine. In love, there is heightened energy and perception of the good within the loved one. As experience deepens and expands your perception, you begin to see beauty everywhere, to love all things, to unite with the divine."

Self-questioning: Is there a person within you that you never show to the world? Can you love her enough to coax her out?

Exercise: Write a list of the ten most influential men (if you are a woman) in your life. Next to each name, write three words describing your feelings about them. What is the "composite personality" of that male within yourself? You will know by the descriptions you have written.

Meditation: Visit the Lovers within yourself, the ones who have attained that perfect union for which you long. Ask for their guidance in your own love relationship. What is it you need to know in order to be more blissfully together? How can you harmonize the opposites within yourself? Listen to what they tell you.

Visualization: Realizing that you have the opposite sex within you, visualize your "other half" and yourself meeting, getting better acquainted, going off together, and making the kind of love for which you have always wished. Be as sensuous and specific as possible.

Astrological Sign: Gemini

Foods: Spice up your life. Prepare a sensuous food feast with flavors and textures galore. Make at least one dish with cayenne or curry; Mexican or East Indian recipes will help. Choose a wine or fresh-squeezed juice to clear the palette. Whole grain breads. Exotic fruit soup or hot miso broth. A smooth creamy pudding. Crunchy crackers with sesame seeds. Whatever strikes your fancy, lay it out, banquet style before you (and your favorite guest). Begin the meal by silence, breathing in the smells of the food. Try feeding each other, hand to mouth, to accentuate the feel of the foods—no talking and no utensils. Avoid the urge to speak, as long as possible. When you must, begin by making only wordless sounds to express your feelings and responses. Let your eyes and actions do the rest.

Colors: Rose, the color of desire and universal love. Warm orange, the color of flesh by candlelight. Golden bangles.

Loving

Oftentimes, the union of the Lovers Within brings about a meeting of your lover in the outer world. Your divine inner partner must be experienced before the outer meeting can take place, though many lovers, temporarily satisfying, may come and go beforehand in order to help you see more clearly the hidden other half of yourself. To encourage the divine lover to come through both your partner and yourself, there are seven simple steps. Once again, follow the path of the tarot.

O The Fool/Seed: Risk presenting to your partner who you really are. This plants the seeds that you want to grow throughout your relationship with another.

1 The Magician/Resources: Utilize to best advantage those

qualities each of you have already developed. Give each other the opportunity to do what each does best. Don't ask each other to do as you do.

2 The High Priestess/Seeker: Take personal responsibility for creating the environment that will promote the type of relationship you want. Practice your part whether or not your partner is practicing his/hers.

3 The Empress/Bounty: Appreciate every kindness done toward you. Each one is a gift. Be outwardly expressive of your thanks.

4 The Emperor/Command: Take command of all of the resources you have within yourself and in your world, and arrange them to benefit you both.

5 The Hierophant/Peacemaker: Make peace by continuing to separate your Self from passing emotions. Do not deepen and expand problems by focusing on them. Instead, concentrate on solutions by using your mind power to create options until you come up with one that pleases you both.

6 The Lovers/Ecstasy: Take time out from your daily routine to love. Sexuality will be more fulfilling to each of you if you offer yourself to one another rather than ask for or require each other's bodily affections. Your soul's beauty is within your body and envelopes it. Offering your body is offering a drink from your soul. Treat it as such and you will always be lovers divine.

7 WARRIOR

Number and Meaning: 7, Rest, success

Traditional Name: Chariot

Medicine Woman Energy: Victorious Warrior

Affirmation: "I am a point of power for the divine plan which works unfailingly through me. Having set my will to follow the highest within, I am strengthened to express the victorious life."

The Card Speaks: "I am the Warrior coming home. Whether you see me on horseback or chariot, know that I am transported by my power to will. I have taken charge of my life and its direction. Your vehicle for movement is symbolic of your mental discipline. It is the personality through which you carry out the Great Plan of Creator Within. Having experienced the energies of cards one through six, you now hold the reins of your life in your own hands. You will have the feeling of being "in the driver's seat" or "at the wheel." Like me, you have been a disciple of the Voice Within, following your own guidance on how to build the structure that is your City of Light. The great discipline that this has required brings you the expertise that enables you to be at ease. You may rest upon this success. The wheels turn now by themselves. You have set in motion the forces that will forever be your foundation.

"Many battles have been won. It is time now to appreciate how far you have come. Feel the security you have created within. Fly with this confidence. You are soaring now, but know that the path will continue to unfold before you. Be ready to take up your shield of power and guard against self-doubt when the next challenge arises. Take full time in this moment to feel the achievement that is presently yours. It will be your foundation; know it well."

Self-questioning: How many powers have you given over to others? Can you grow your own food? Can you teach your own children? Can you make your own clothes? Can you walk five miles? Can you feel comfortable alone? Can you go a day without a cigarette? A cup of coffee? Food? Your car? Clothes? Make-up? Money?

Exercise: Take over a function that you have given over to others.

Meditation: Dwell on your accomplishments. No matter how far you have to go to find them, do not allow the mind to interfere by reminding you of any failures.

Visualization: Visualize a vehicle (chariot, horse, boat, or whatever you would like to ride on) taking you toward your next experience of success. Discover where it takes you. Experience every detail of this next plateau. See your friends congratulating you. Perhaps they will be preparing a banquet. Just follow the path and see.

Astrological Sign: Cancer

Foods: In each person's life, there come to be certain foods that symbolize "success." It may be champagne and caviar, a steak dinner, a complete meal from your own garden or, for some, the ability to eat no meal at all. Whatever would bring you the feelings of "success," indulge in it now. Throw off any associated guilts temporarily and allow the fantasy to take you in, at least for a day, completely. Notice any changes in the way you perceive yourself and others as you indulge in "success."

Colors: Brilliant orange-yellow for the power of mind and being that radiates from you. Wear the clothing of accomplishment.

The Valley

It is important to remember that success is not a static state. You must enjoy the moment and allow yourself to continue forward even though, as in a mountain climb, after the peak there is but to descend. If you can be wise enough to foresee the valley you are approaching from your vantage point at the pinnacle, you will prepare and act accordingly. Compared to the climb, a rest is ahead.

Life keeps you moving on. Trust yourself. The Chariot/Warrior is only card 7. There are many experiences ahead. You can enjoy them if you don't fight to stay here at this particular peak. A warrior seldom becomes great by fighting one battle. Your skills must be constantly honed. Your retreat is as important as your advance. Take time to regroup, to become re-inspired. Celebrate the victory, make it yours, take it inside yourself, then relax. Tomorrow will start a new period.

8 HEALING

Number and Meaning: 8, Harmony, balance

Traditional Name: Strength

Medicine Woman Energy: Healing Power

Affirmation: "All of my desires have aligned with my highest ideals, thus my presence heals. I look forward with confidence to the eternal splendor of my love-filled life."

The Card Speaks: "Strength is the quality present in me when my mind and heart are working in the same direction. I have learned how to place my desires, like a chain of roses, one intertwined with another, in a mutually compatible arrangement. I have rejected those desires that interfere with my main purpose in life, and I have seen how my talents and abilities, my deep felt longings and soul needs can all work together for my highest good. I have learned to use my creative imagination, trying out different arrangements, until I see how I can transform what appears to be an obstacle into a benefactor.

"I have tamed the beast. What were once threatening forces I now control through the power of my thought. Not by creating walls, but by making of the enemy a friend, do I gain dominion. My power is the power of the caring ways. I possess the power of my inner convictions. My sexual/life/creative energy is channeled, through the thoughts which I dwell upon, toward the upliftment of others in service to the One.

"I live within you. As you work with changing the patterns of your own life, becoming conscious of your choices, you feel me grow. The energy I have to give to you is infinite. Only the mind interferes by its limiting thoughts. As you change them, you open the door to my unbounded love and healing force."

Self-questioning: What would happen if I stopped complaining?

Exercise: Make a list of all that you desire (both qualities and things). See how one can lead to another. Arrange them in a hierarchy. Don't expect to do this exercise any faster than you can put together a jigsaw puzzle.

Meditation: Imagine yourself ready to take a journey to a Garden of Paradise where there awaits the Healing Woman, Strength. Call upon her, visualize her, then listen to her speak to you. Do not judge her words, thinking you are "only making them up." Refrain from telling yourself, "This can't be true." Listen until there is a feeling of completeness. Analyze what has been said *only* when you are through. You may question her during the speaking, but be sure to listen to and accept her answers. She is waiting to talk to you, depending for her existence on your willingness to give her form in your mind.

Visualization: Picture someone you love. For twenty minutes, send that person loving thoughts in any way you can. If this person has asked for healing, see them healed. Later, don't ask them if they felt it, simply observe any changes in them over the next few weeks.

Astrological Sign: Leo

Foods: Foods are nature's healers. Many books have been written on healing diets. Sometimes these diets and theories seem to conflict with each other, causing confusion in the one struggling to find the "right" way of eating. All

naturally healing diets, however, emphasize the importance of fresh whole foods. Locally grown, nonchemicalized
foods should make up the main part of your health-pro-
ducing daily diet. When wondering about specific substances—"Is this food/herb/drink right for me in this
particular moment?"—try the muscle test.

To begin the muscle test, make an agreement with your
body/mind that if a substance is good for you, you will be
stronger. Place one arm out to the side, level with your
shoulder. Have a friend push down after telling you to
"resist." You will notice your strength or weakness. Then
place the substance in question in your other hand over the
solar plexus or in your mouth and repeat the test. Are you
stronger or weaker? If weaker, try tasting something whole-
some (this will differ from person to person) until you get
a "stronger" response, just to prove to yourself that it wasn't
tiredness that made you weaker. A more thorough explanation of muscle testing can be found in *Your Body Doesn't
Lie* by John Diamond, M.D.

Colors: Wear green for healing and balance. Blue for
calming and anesthetizing. Yellow for cheer. Visualize
orange flowing through the body for healing of skin. Try
red when feeling depressed or weak. Wear a particular
color for three to seven days and you will clearly see how
it affects you both emotionally and physically.

Healing Strength

If you get 8 Healing in a reading, it is probably telling you
that you must be a healing force in the situation. You may
have to work behind the scenes, but it is *your* consciousness that has the superior power to create a beneficial
outcome.

You must keep your mind in the light. Make sure you are envisioning potential success, whether it be health, wealth, or conflict resolution. Your inner force is strong and can see you through whatever trouble might be appearing. In fact, it may be so strong right now that you don't even see any trouble. All the better.

Your state of high consciousness will automatically be resolving difficulties all around you without your even working at it. This is the strength of your bright inner vision. Let it continue to fill you with thoughts of love and beauty and these vibrations will radiate from you quite naturally. It is this card of strength and healing that is best expressed in the Blessingway prayer below.

I will be happy forever
Nothing will hinder me
I walk with beauty before me
I walk with beauty behind me
I walk with beauty above me
I walk with beauty below me
I walk with beauty around me
My words will be beautiful

This is a prayer of the Navajo people. Visualize and inwardly feel the beauty of life surrounding you as you say it. The more you radiate healing, the stronger your healing force will become. Walk in beauty.

9 GUIDE

Number and Meaning: 9, Completion, foundation

Traditional Name: The Hermit

Medicine Woman Energy: The Guide on the Path Up the Mountain

Affirmation: "I and my High Self are one. I stand alone on the sure foundation of eternal Being, lighting the way for others who come behind me."

The Card Speaks: "You have sought freedom, and now you have realized that freedom comes through working to achieve inner perfection not through seeking fame and fortune. You have completed the basic work. You have laid the foundation for that which will be the manifestation of God in Earth through your Self. I, the Hermit within you, long hidden away in the dark caverns of your being, have come forth as the Guide to light your way upon the path to the Great Being. You have seen the 'light at the end of the tunnel.' You have found the Teacher Within.

"The first part of the path you walk 'alone.' Now, I am with you. You have touched a place within yourself, you might call it a certain degree of comfort and confidence that feels like 'home.' There is a drawing within to be nourished, to drink deeply of the well of divine inspiration. The goal has become the source. You (I) and the Spirit are One. This is the moment of heavenly ecstasy.

"With me, you are secure within yourself, able to keep silent among those who will not understand. Your healthy instincts have led you to the right books, people, and situations. You have listened to the word of God within others' speaking. And you have heeded my voice as I encouraged you through your intuition.

"I live in simplicity, humbly, in mental stillness, like the pond deep within the forest. I await those who will follow. The vibration of the seeker enters my awareness like a falling leaf. When I hear the footsteps on the path, I light the way. Come with me now, and we will continue our journey together."

Self-questioning: Do I now seek the Spirit with my whole heart?

Exercise: 1. For one day, drink only juices; eat no food. 2. For one day, do not speak. 3. Be alone for twenty-four hours straight. These may all be done at once, on the same day, if you wish.

Meditation: Preferably on the same day as one or more of the exercises are performed, prepare yourself physically through yoga, exercise, dance, or any other movement that feels appropriate. Do not eat for a few hours before you begin. Prepare a special space in your room where you cannot be disturbed for an hour or so. You might light incense, bring flowers or a candle. Prepare as if expecting a special guest. Do all of this for your Guide, trusting that even though you may not be ready to see him/her, s/he will be there. Give the Guide permission to move through your ego barriers, to touch you more deeply than ever before. Expect nothing. Just remain in a receptive, relaxed mood after acknowledging your readiness. At the end of the hour, give thanks for *whatever* happened.

Visualization: Make up a Wise Person in your mind's eye, one who knows all about you. Then have this person talk to you about your present life situation. It often helps to write yourself a letter, as if written by this person.

Astrological Sign: Virgo

Foods: For this day, take special care to prepare everything ceremoniously. You are serving a very High Being within yourself. Use your best tableware, the highest quality food, a pleasing setting. Make it a very special occasion. And have exactly what you really want. Eat slowly, savoring every bite. Eat exactly how much you want. Allow nothing to interfere, no thoughts, no reprimands, no "shoulds" or "should nots."

Colors: Surround yourself with everything that brings you "home." Warm, brown, earthy tones, warm reds and oranges, yellow greens, golden, fiery light. Wear loose, comfortable clothes that allow your body its freedom to move. Be guided from within.

Is This My Guide?

There are several questions that often arise in regard to the concept of spirit Guides. One is, "Are they real?" It is common to discount your imagination as something frivolous and to believe yourself to be "making things up." My response, first of all, is to tell you that if you can "make up things" that result in profound inner changes that create happy lives and change the world, that is "real" enough.

I cannot convince your rational mind that Guides are real. Only your experience over time will tell you. However, belief in Guides as separate entities is not necessary in order for you to progress spiritually.

To me, the Guides are quite real, much more real than the ever-changing human-made world. But I have taken a long road to this understanding. Your personal Guide will lead you through experiences that will bring you to the exact sense of knowing what is right for you at just the time you need it. The first lesson by the Guide that you are being taught, however, is to trust yourself. Trust your own inner experience. Your self-confidence in your own spiritual journey is what builds the bridge to working with the Higher Beings. Their hands reach out to those who sincerely seek. If you seek to live truth, higher love, and compassion, then you prepare yourself for meeting those who exemplify those virtues.

Another question often asked is, "Why would such High Beings wish to spend time with me?" It is their particular area of universal service and personal evolution to help the Earth and her beings. They come to you according to your readiness and willingness to work with them. It is important for you to remember that they do want to *work* with you. They give guidance so that it can be carried out. The Guide will, of course, *never* tell you to do anything against your moral principles, but may ask you to transcend some of your limitations about how much good it is possible for you to accomplish.

"How will I know if it is really my Guide, not a lower spirit perhaps of someone recently deceased and still earth-bound?" you may ask. Your Guide will be able to transmit total love to you; an overwhelming feeling of cosmic blessing or grace will emanate from hir presence. And, you can rightly ask, "Are you my Guide?" All spirits on the other side are bound to truth. And you have the power to instantaneously dismiss any unwelcome spirit just by telling it to go away and giving it no further attention.

Secondly, your Guide will direct you toward one life purpose. S/he will not change hir mind about what that is. S/he will be glad to answer questions and provide details as you need them. The Guide is a guide. S/he is not the culmination of your journey to the Godhead, but an important way-shower and bringer of love, acceptance, forgiveness, and boundless inspiration toward more and more wondrous realms. You are certain to fall in love with hir. Don't be afraid to build the bridge of imagination so that she may find hir way to you.

10 HARVEST

Number and Meaning: 10, Manifestation

Traditional Name: Wheel of Fortune

Medicine Woman Energy: The Season's Harvest

Affirmation: "All that I have allowed to dwell in my imagination has become true through my words and actions. The Creator is embodied in me. I gratefully accept the harvest of my creation."

The Card Speaks: "You have heard it spoken: 'The Word has become flesh and dwells among us.' The words you have kept in your mind, for good or evil, have come into material form. The images you have dwelled on have become real. That which you have imaged-in has come into actual being. In the beginning was the word you held in your mind, spoke through your mouth, and now the son of that word is here. The word is embodied in your flesh. Whatsoever you have sown, so will you reap. That time is now. I am the Wheel of Life, the turning of the seeds you have sown. You may count on me to bring 'good luck' if you have listened and followed levels (cards) 0 through 9. I am the Law of Karma. You have put your energy out into the world in certain ways—these include thoughts as well as actions—and now, whatever you have given returns.

This is the rhythm of life. This is the rhythm of emotion. Anger begets anger. Joy begets joy.

"One cycle is completed. You have now experienced in fullness a certain aspect of your life. If you have done your inner work, a desire has been realized. A new step in your spiritual journey will unfold before you now.

"You began the wheel of fortune spinning when you took a gamble. As the Fool, you stepped into new territory. You tried using your present personality and environment in some new ways as the Magician. As the High Priestess, you began to see yourself as a causal force. Then, as Empress, you looked with love upon the person full of potential that you are. As Emperor, you began to make a structure to put that potential to work. Listening to the Voice Within, the Hierophant, you figured out just how to interface with the world. Working together, you became Lovers with your Inner World, bringing it into outer manifestation. In the Chariot, you experienced your accomplishment. Then you built up your inner strength until you could stand alone and steady as the Hermit lighting the way for others who follow. This is the turning of the Wheel of Tarot. I bring you the results of this whole energy cycle. Your task now is to accept. Rejoice. Be glad in what is. And go on. Just as the gambler might have a drink 'to the game' after a round of cards, whether s/he won or lost, celebrate now just because you have come this far. Give a toast to the flow. Shake hands with your friends for a game well-played.

"As a Medicine Woman, you understand now that the seeds you gave to the wind, through your nurturing, have grown into the food that nourishes yourself. You have used the tools at hand, seeking vision from within as to how to take these everyday things and make them work for you. You looked and listened to Earth, your environment. You took command of your resources. You carried in your heart the vibration of peace, seeking the good of the whole. Through your loving action, you found a Great Spirit which then flowed through you as you moved through the challenges you encountered. Your imagining power of mind, like a strong horse, carried you through the strongest opposition. In your wisdom, you called on the healing forces, and guidance came to you. Now, you rest. This is the way of the Medicine Woman (cards 0 through 10). This is the journey of the Medicine Wheel."

Self-questioning: Do I allow myself to rest after my cycle of work? Do I accept what I have done after I have done it? Or do I use this time to criticize myself?

Exercise: Make a "Wheel of Fortune" by drawing a circle, dividing it into the major areas of your life, such as health, relationships, work, spirituality, enjoyment, or whatever categories you prefer to use. Then, find magazine photos or draw in those images of things you would like to see happen through you in the next six months of time. (Note that I said "through" you, not "to" you.) Put the Wheel of Fortune where you will notice it every day. The images will implant in your subconscious and seemingly without effort begin to draw you into situations and learnings which will bring about the results you have imaged-in.

Meditation: Imagine that you are sitting before a large Wheel of Fortune. Give it a spin and see if the jackpot is yours today. If you are "off the mark," ask what is interfering with your good luck.

Visualization: In your easy and relaxed way, begin to daydream of all the good, fortunate things you have wished for and received. Make your images clear, detailed, and colorful. Let yourself see how much you have harvested. See the support you have been given by various people around you. See how your gifts have helped others in their own lives. Allow the richness of your resources to become clear. Then give the mental command that your ability to draw to yourself the things, people, and situations you desire is increasing daily and that your desires are ever constantly aligning with the greatest good for all. Enjoy.

Astrological Sign: Jupiter

Food: If you were wise enough to plant a garden, now is your time to reap the harvest. Prepare a feast of foods you have nurtured in love and feel the warmth and energy they return to you.

Colors: Violet is the ray that clears "old karma." It has been called the "cosmic eraser." Whether you wear it or meditate on it, its action is to clean out the molasses of confused thinking and limiting beliefs and make space in your body cells to hold the Light.

The Medicine Wheel

There are Medicine Wheels of various kinds in every ancient tradition. Though they may be laid out in stone or known only inwardly, the sacred circles teach the laws of life. A wheel turns. What you place at one point comes back to you later. The Wheel of Fortune as we know it in the games of chance seems to bring us unexpected good fortune or loss. But the truth is, though it may be unexpected, it is not entirely unpredictable. It is just that usually by the time the results come in, we have long since forgotten our initial output and its connection to those results.

The *Medicine Woman Inner Guidebook* works with the Four Powers Medicine Wheel, a multi-level circle of physical, emotional, mental, and spiritual energies that flow through you strongly at particular times of the year.

In the North direction, the Wheel is at Winter, a time that quite naturally turns your focus to how well you have prepared yourself materially for winter weather. Is your home secure? Your wood in? Your car battery charged? Is there food stored for the long, cold season? Even if you do not live in a cold climate or have to provide your own food and heat from your direct manual labor, these urges are primal. There are still preparations to make for the out-growth of spring if you want to have the greatest sense of renewal when that season arrives.

In the East, Spring rises. It is the energy of dawn, of inspiration, hope, excitement, new adventure. It is a sexual time, a creative time, an uplifting, renewing, spiritually exciting time. Your energy quite naturally goes outward to new pursuits, new people. You want to plant, whether you plant seeds for flowers, food, or future fun. The whole Earth is saying, "Now is the time."

In the South, Summer is upon us. This is when your garden flourishes. Every seed you have planted emotion-ally, your wishes and desires, must be carefully watered by a clear mind. You are to weed your mind of thoughts that interfere with growth and maturity of those things you started in Spring. No abandoning ship here unless you want to lose the harvest. It is a time for sorting out, planning, and developing. You carry toward maturity those things you began in your spring inspiration stage.

Fall, at the West gate of the Wheel, will show you what you have done. Your labors will bear fruit and that which needs to be put to rest will be destroyed. Fall will find you fine-tuning your relationships and getting ready for a long, cozy winter, if you understand that the Wheel asks you to prepare for the time forthcoming.

If you pay no attention to the cycles and seasons of life and the energies they call into play, you will be constantly surprised, and not always happily, with what "Lady Luck" brings you. Find your place on the Wheel and attend to energies it is calling from you now.

11 BALANCE

Number and Meaning: 11, Balance

Traditional Name: Justice

Medicine Woman Energy: The Restoration of Nature's Balance

Affirmation: "Divine Justice works within me, eliminating all that is unnecessary from my thoughts and granting to me all that is good. I walk in balance, knowing Earth's care."

The Card Speaks: "I, Balance, as a Universal Force, have many things to consider. I must look through Time, judging the effect of present actions on future generations. I work through you, presenting opportunities that would benefit many, if you choose to heed my call. I speak through what some have referred to as your 'conscience,' giving you *in any moment* an immediate sense of what is right or wrong action on your part. I never work as Guilt, though I am sometimes mistaken for this one. I am more correctly experienced as Enthusiasm or Hesitation, depending on the situation at hand and whether the action you contemplate would benefit or harm the whole. Guilt, on the other hand, is often a conglomeration of old rules spoken to you by others and being held in your mind as 'shoulds' or 'shouldn'ts.' I, instead, work only in the *now*. I am your immediate pre-action response to the situation at hand.

"I want you to act. It is only through you that my work is done. Likewise, it is only through your action that *you* know if your inner convictions are truly in the good of the whole. You must test out your theories. You must see if they are valid. Your inner sense will tell you *in the moment* if you are creating balance . . . harmony . . . equilibrium. That which you no longer need, whether theories or things, will in this way be eliminated. My sword will fall, cutting away those thoughts that limit you. You will give away any possessions that are weighing you down. You will break away from people or circumstances that no longer promote your growth.

"I am the archetype of self-discipline. With me, you will begin to pursue enthusiastically your self-direction. Justice will prevail. True balance will begin. Remember, I am accountable for the whole Earth. What is allowed in your life must balance out through time and for all life forms. Everything affects the whole. As you work with an awareness of this and of me, you will find a great peace overcoming your life."

Self-questioning: How you value (what value you place on) your experience (each one of them) decrees how that experience will live within you, whether as a burden or as an inspiration. How much dead weight do you carry? Resentments, grudges, shoulds, shouldn'ts . . . these are heavy responses. Forgiveness is Light. Joy is Light. Kindness is Light.

Exercise: This week, give away one thing that you no longer need.

Meditation: For seven days, monitor your thoughts and words. Notice every time you use negativity or indulge in "ain't it awful" down and out chitchat. When you become aware of this going on, *be silent*, or change your words to the most positive ones you can still believe to be true. This is called a mental diet and is an active ongoing conscious form of meditation. If you can stay on this diet for one week, you will find a great deal of heaviness lifted from your life.

Visualization: Image-in yourself holding the scales of balance. On one side, place something you *have*. On the other side, place what you *give* in exchange for this. Is there balance?

Astrological Sign: Libra

Colors: Green is the color of perfect balance. Use it freely in healing. Eat it. Wear it. Visualize it. Surround yourself with nature's green. A lack of green money in your life may mean that your society is out of balance in terms of respect for nature's green, growing life. You are only a portion of that larger balance or imbalance. At any given moment, your life experience is giving you opportunity to restore the greater balance and thereby your own.

Lessons of Balance

Right now, we live in a world very unbalanced on a large scale. The resources of the Earth have been mined unremittingly with little done to replenish and restore. The Earth will adjust. One of her options is to destroy old land masses and create new ones. The destruction may occur where humans have most harmed her. Or she may allow "innocent victims" to go under with the changes in order to activate compassion and set up new priorities in the hearts of the remaining humans. The Earth is a powerful being and though humans have often worked against her power, she is still very able to eliminate species, including us, from her body.

We are entirely dependent on her for material existence. Her wood, metal, air, water, and fire are the basis of absolutely everything. Humans find this easiest to forget when they, individually, do not have to go to her directly for these supplies. The factories and stores are seen as suppliers of all our needs. However, all factories and stores are supplied by a larger being: Earth.

Does it not make sense, then, to seek ways to work *with* her powers, to replenish her resources. She is most generous with seeds. There is only space needed for planting and compost—the return to her of all waste matter—needed for nourishment. We must stop producing poisons, toxic waste, unregenerative garbage that she cannot transform without killing us in the process.

Justice will be done. It is a prime spiritual force. But if we are polluter and polluted, we may have to be that which is destroyed so that others may live. Let us change now, instead, to work as keepers of the land, as lovers of the beauty she offers, as healers with her herbs and foods, as stewards of the great garden, and as Gods and Goddesses of her everlasting fertility.

Foods to Balance Your Being

The Spirit affects the Mind. The Mind affects the Emotions. The Emotions affect the body. The body is the dwelling place of the Spirit.

You have a great power over the food you eat and its effect on your body. Try the muscle test: Have a friend stand in front of you. Raise your arm straight out to the side from the shoulder (parallel to the floor). Have the friend press down firmly for a few seconds to test your resistance to the pressure. You resist as much as possible. The point here is to simply give a check as to how strong you are at this particular moment. Now take a food you believe to be "bad for you" and hold it in your mouth while your friend asks you to resist once more and again makes the muscle check by pressing down on your forearm. (The pressing down should be just long enough to get an immediate reading of stronger or weaker.) You were probably a little weaker this time.

Now, before you take another mouthful of the same food, sincerely bless the food. You may use a traditional grace before meals, or your own words of love and respect for the food. Ask it to please promote your health and vitality. Then take the food in your mouth while your friend muscle tests in the same way s/he did before. I have seen this test used with the "worst" of foods and found that the blessing always vitalized the food enough to make the person strong once again.

So, thank your food for being here for you. Appreciate and accept the life within it. Take into yourself, mentally affirming, only the health and nutrition it can supply. This is a blessing that you give and will receive back into yourself within the food as you eat it.

Affirm in your mind the idea that what you are eating is good for you. You can't pretend here. If you have strong underlying beliefs that it is really bad for you, you will only cause conflict within yourself. You can, however, work on changing the old beliefs by seeking out new information that your intellect will "buy." Using the muscle test and/or a pendulum as a biofeedback device is a great aid in giving the mind visible proof of whether something is or is not good for your body at a particular time.

During meals, surround yourself in serenity, away from disturbance. The emotions should be still while ingesting food, except for the feeling of enjoyment in the meal.

On the physical level, eat the freshest, most whole—that is, closest to the natural state—foods available. Whenever possible, eat the foods that are in season and grown close to home. This keeps your vibration in tune with your environment.

You might want to clip the following verse and put it on your refrigerator to remind you of these lessons.

Sun is the first food,
Fresh air and water second.
Rest, exercise, and laughter
Nourish you third.
Fourth, the seed of the Earth brings life.
Fifth, the herb, vegetable, and fruit give health.
And sixth, if these be lacking,
The animals will provide.

Cast aside as little as you can
From these, the gifts that nourish.
This, in thanksgiving for their being.
Be positive and kind in preparation,
Friendly and serene in consuming,
Joyful and active in digestion,
And health will be your inner light.

Eat from nature, if you can,
The herbs and wild foods provided.
Garden by organic means or purchase
The least affected, neglected, processed,
    and imperfected.
Locally grown helps you be tuned to home.
Above all, envision
Radiant vitality to be your own.

The Food Rainbow

White	Milk, the food of the Mother
Violet, Indigo, Blue	Berries and fruits, growing high off the ground, reaching for Spirit
Green	Vegetables and weeds of the sea, healing me
Yellow	Grains, eggs, cheese, butter, and oils, golden gifts of sustenance
Orange	Carrots, pumpkins, and squash, citrus and melons, rich in the power of life
Red	Beets, beans, nuts, seeds, basic building blocks of life
Brown	And if there is a need to ground the self, to stabilize and warm the fragile body, cook the foods in the blessings of fire.

Cooking and eating can be a ritual of love for Mother Earth, Spirit, and Self. The more you appreciate and bless your food, the more it will bless you. If you eat from the rainbow of life-giving substances, you will seldom have to deal with illness.

If you are habituated to cigarettes, coffee, alcohol, medical or nonmedical drugs, or sugar and highly processed, chemicalized foods, begin to replace them one by one with a food from the rainbow of life. Every time you indulge in an old habit-substance, do it in a prayerful way, such as:

"Creator within me, I offer you this habit that it might lead me to transformation. I bless this substance for what it has given me and ask to be easily and quickly shown that which must now replace it. I trust that you have something much better in store for me. I choose life-giving ways now and release all that leads me to illness or death. I bless this substance knowing that this may be my final interaction with it. Thank you."

One of the worst parts of substance abuse or any addiction, no matter how mild, is the self-chastisement that often accompanies it. Begin to replace guilt with an empowering emotion so that your courage can be built up once again. Your habit was acquired because it was the only choice available within your previous life conditions. So let yourself off the hook. And begin now to make one small increment of change.

Eating well, becoming healthy and whole, brings accompanying peaceful emotional states and allows you to go to higher states of consciousness. If you don't like yourself, feed the Goddess within you, that spark of eternal life that causes your ongoing existence. When well-fed, she will begin to take over and to draw to you the life fit for a Goddess, and you will be living it.

12 VISION

Number and Meaning: 12, Complete immersion

Traditional Name: The Hanged Man

Medicine Woman Energy: The Vision Quest Fulfilled

Affirmation: "I surrender to the greater good. The Great Spirit and I are one. The beauty I see, I will bring through me."

The Card Speaks: "Receiving the vision of that which is to be my purpose and my work on the Earth, I am able to surrender to the greater good. I give up my life of thinking that I am a separate ego that must maintain myself at the expense of others. I am within others. Others are within me.

"I no longer care so much whether I am understood by others, but whether I understand them. My ego needs align with the Great Plan. My wants are in harmony with the human longing for perfection. Creating my own small spot of paradise on Earth adds to the Great Creation. There is no longer a conflict. I serve myself and others at the same time.

"My face is without pain, though others would have thought that to sacrifice the ego (consciousness of separateness) would be to suffer. Instead, my aura glows. There is no strain in this reversal of thinking. I hang from the Tree of Life, still growing. The horizontal plane of the cross symbolizes my work on the Earth. The vertical plane is my alignment with God. I now look at life from a different perspective than ever before. I am able to see things from another's point of view. I am able to look with the eyes of

God. My individuality is simply a tool, a point of focus for the universal Will-to-Good. Life, as I once knew it, has been turned upside down. The Good of the Whole is my highest goal. I have looked deep within the waters of consciousness and have been transformed."

Self-questioning: As I look at the day just passed, did I consider the good of my whole Self in my decisions? The good of my whole environment? The good of the whole group? The good of my whole community? Or only the good of one small aspect of my Self?

Exercise: Sit across from a partner (someone you would like to be close to). Relax and look deeply into the other's eyes while the eyes remain still, neither blinking nor moving from side to side. In a few moments, close them. Then imagine yourself going inside the other person's body. Become the person. Look out the other person's eyes, seeing yourself. Now think of yourself as that partner you are within right now. How does s/he see you? How does s/he see the world? What does it feel like to be in that body? What does s/he need from you? What are her/his hopes or fears? Now come back into your own body. Still with eyes closed, allow the deeper essence of that person to flow toward you by making a connection of light from your heart, throat, and third eye to a point between the two of you. Just be there, receiving. Begin to open to the God-ness. When it feels right, draw all of your energies gently back into yourself. Feel your own God-ness. Follow the flow.

Meditation: Go to your highest space of meditation. From this peak, look down upon the world. What do you see needing to be done? This is your work.

Visualization: See yourself as a channel of heavenly gifts.

For a time, you hold the gifts, adding your individual energy to them. Then, one by one, you pass them on to others. See the effects of your giving to others.

Astrological Sign: Neptune

Surrender

To become the vision received from the Greater Being, you must surrender to your greater Self. You must take the leap of faith, letting go of things on which you have formerly depended. This may include an old self-image, self-doubt, or embarrassment at who you really are.

You must dive into the unknown. The person who goes into the wilderness on vision quest leaves behind the comforts of hir former home. S/he often refrains from eating or sleeping and sees no other humans or the things of humans. S/he is left to view that which comes from within. This inner space reveals itself in outer reality. The inner being becomes the world.

Often, at first, a level of fears is manifest. The ego, which I like to call the "personality self," lets you know just what would devour it. It is up to you to let it be devoured. In the process, you will come to realize that it is you, the Greater Self, who devours it.

The Vision (Hanged Man) card is different from the Seed, or Fool, in that the Fool steps blindly forward on a hunch or a feeling, often not realizing what s/he is leaving behind, whereas the Hanged Man questing for vision purposely lets go of the known for what s/he sees ahead as hir destiny.

The Fool might ask you every day to step forward, take a risk, plant a seed. The Vision card is just to remind you of the one turnabout that must occur. Your life, at some point, must be given to the Ultimate Being-Consciousness-

Bliss that resides beyond the mind and its busy-ness. Your daily actions may continue, but the quest is no longer for direct results from those actions. You are simply allowing a greater force to work through you, as it surely will when you have surrendered.

It is a force that was always within you, but hidden by the personality's goals. The personality remains, but it is now doing God's work rather than its own. Vision asks you not to give up "you," but to become more than you, the one Self that animates all life.

You can seek vision and prepare for vision, but you cannot force it to come. It is a gift. When you receive it, it will turn your life upside down. As if diving from a cliff for the first time, you cannot know what complete immersion is like until you are fully in the water. Only then can you swim. Only then can you act in accordance with the new element that surrounds you.

Surrender is not death, but action within a new environment of higher consciousness. It is *not* giving up the personality of self to another human's Will. This is a very important distinction. The meaning of the vision card is an inner experience of God as complete motivation of the Self. It is not a surrender to any other human being. The personality will still function quite strongly, able to stand up for itself in the world perhaps even more than ever before. The vision is the Prime Mover, an energy source that will prompt all future actions and guide your way for the rest of your life.

The Vision card will come up again and again only for you to further fine-tune your carrying out of the original vision given to you by the Great Spirit. It will not *change* your basic vision. This card focuses your life within God's perfect plan. Pay attention to what you know you are on Earth to do.

13 SUNSET

Number and Meaning: 13, Transformation

Traditional Name: Death

Medicine Woman Energy: The Ride through the Desert toward the Setting Sun

Affirmation: "I accept the changes that will come through higher states of consciousness. All change works to bring about my freedom and my good. I let go and am free."

The Card Speaks: "Like the setting sun, I am Death to that which has been of this day; yet I promise renewal. When there is no other way out, I come. I am kind. Only I can offer the opportunity to leave behind the unsolvable problems. I am firm. There is no return to what has been. Through me, you are called to the Creator. You are called to listen once more to the Great Plan and the part you must play in it. I am the end of life as you have known it. I am the beginning of what you have not yet imagined.

"When you see me coming, open to change. I am a warning. I tell you that the patterns through which you are working are leading to your end. In your body, I am constantly taking the old cells to make room for the new. Every few years, your body is totally recreated in the form of your thoughts. You create the body through your intellectual patterns. Change the pattern (the thought and image) and you change the form. Restructuring the mind is restructuring the body.

"In your world, I bring change as the people change. All social change comes from the death of old bodies—em-

93

bodiments of ways of thinking—and the birth of new. In this way, opportunities for liberation are constantly provided.

"Death is change at the basic structural level. You can change your body and your experience through new concepts. Everything realigns as your thoughts take a new order. Every good (God) thought that you dwell on creates light in the cell until it can be truly said, 'The kingdom of God is within,' 'The Goddess lives again through me.'

"Fear of death is fear of change, fear that your good will not come. Fear of Death is fear of the law (the equivalent of the word 'Lord'). The law is: As you think, so will you be. Fear is overcome by love. Thinking love-thoughts fills your being with love. Realizing that every change brings you an opportunity to renew allows you to see the beauty of the plan, the divine order, in all movement. Just seeing that every death/renewal *is* your growth lets you begin to rest in love, to feel love not as a syrupy emotion but as a deep appreciation, a gladness at another chance to change your mind. Fear of the Law/Lord/Mind (all the same thing) changes to using the Law of Mind, filling the mind with appreciation of change, evolution, opportunity to review and renew. This is the perfect love that casts out fear. Fear of death is overcome by this wisdom.

"As the sun sets each day, I ask you, have you taken this opportunity to change? Have you used this day to grow in love, to fulfill your purpose? If not, I will be coming around again. I will appear more and more ominous, as you need. I will strike fear into your heart, if that is what it takes. For I am kind. And if you use the power of your life, I will come only when all is done, to bring you gentle respite . . . to escort you on to higher places . . . to lead you to the One."

Self-questioning: Am I taking the opportunities for growth that are presented to me? Or do I wait until I am pushed by a difficult situation? Do I learn by going ahead into more love, more creativity, or do I wait for struggle to be my teacher?

Exercise: Write a two-page paper describing your own death.

Meditation: Allow yourself to imagine rising up out of your body. Knowing that you are connected by a lifeline that is strong and vibrant, tell your body/mind that, just for a few minutes, you would like to review your "death." Assure yourself that you will not *really* die, that this is merely an exercise in awareness. Then observe your death and the situation, feelings, insights, surrounding it.

Visualization: See Death as a person, coming to speak with you about your life and purpose. Follow Death riding into the sunset until you get the message you need.

Astrological Sign: Scorpio

Colors: Black is a color often associated with Death. Black is a color that absorbs all, just as death absorbs all. Black is also associated with Earth, for it is Earth from which our bodies have come. How do you feel in black?

A Death Ritual

Something, someone, some part of you has died. Let us create a ritual of transformation so that the energy and matter that was bound up in that old way of being can be released. It is released into the greater reality to be worked with by the Gods and Goddesses of love and wisdom. It will be reformed into something potentially more useful, more in harmony with now, more beneficial to humankind.

Let us give thanks. For all it has been, for all it meant to us, for its comfort, friendship, the discipline it took to keep it, we give thanks. For our opportunity to depend on it, lean on it, use it, we give thanks. For our chance to serve it, love it, embrace it, we give thanks. Let us recognize that it worked for us and we learned from it.

Then let us move on. We let go of all that we didn't like about it by forgiving and getting rid of all reminders that connect us to negative memories and emotions. We free ourselves from the limitation it put on us. The mementos we keep are only those which allow us to revere and appreciate what the dead meant to us. Articles of devotion, that is all we keep. And in these, we see that we love God through them, that it was some quality of God, of greatness, of beauty, of transcendence that we saw in the lost other. And that quality is now within us. All that we needed to learn from the now gone has been internalized in our Self. The dead lives but is transformed by our very union with it.

Let us continue. Our life proceeds, ever enriched by this knowing. Our kingdom comes. We now carry the lessons, the learning, the qualities. Our will carries on. It is our chance to do better, to be higher, to place into Earth that which is in Heaven. Our daily sustenance is the food of this past. We forgive our thoughtlessness in regard to these gifts which now are only memories. We lift the veils which have fallen upon our present lives in order to see where now we can more fully live in thanksgiving for what is. For here is our place, our moment, our opportunity for peace, our chance to love. Here, now is our kingdom, our will which is free.

Death, we give thanks, has lifted a weight, a burden, has freed a complex of energy to be turned into Light. I open to this Light and walk the sacred way as it shines upon me.

So be it in this day.

14 BLEND

Number and Meaning: 14, Integration

Traditional Name: Temperance

Medicine Woman Energy: The Rainbow's Blend

Affirmation: "The Inner Alchemist mixes everything I have ever known, thought, or said into a perfect blend. Order is easily bestowed on my life experience."

The Card Speaks: "I am the rainbow, calling you to relax and allow the perfect blending of all that is within you. I am the mixer of the beautiful elixir. My colors create all that is your world. In you, I work to create a clarity of thinking that will lead you to the Ultimate Union with the One. I combine your ideas, ideals, and experiences into an arrow of truth and aim it at the only target. Let me do my work.

"Everything in the universe is vibration, and vibration can be changed by your mental state. Meditation, concentration, reflection, relaxation . . . all change your vibration. This is the Divine mixing, blending, tempering of your experience. You have acted, you have tried, now you must integrate the experience with everything else that is you. I help you to see where it all fits, how things have been changed and how they can be used.

"Remember, experience is the test of ideas. In your practice, shoot at some definite mark. Accept no theories until you have tested them out. Life is your opportunity to *try*, not to *accept*. Act and then evaluate. Go toward the promise at the rainbow's end. You, as an individual, choose your direction, your every action; yet you are indivisible from the Whole. The Cosmic Will works through you; yet you must assume total responsibility for every thought and action. You are guided, you have a mission and a purpose; yet you function with complete free will, as an independent agent. You are constantly channeling the Universal Life Force into the world through your patterns of thought and image.

"You are the actor. I am the integrator of your actions. Take time for me. Temperance, the Divine Blending, happens automatically whenever you relax."

Self-questioning: Am I always too busy? Do I allow time for the necessary integration of all of my experiences?

Exercise: Take three hours off, completely. Do not include in the three hours preparation time, driving time, and so on. Go away from your usual environment to a place where you can relax alone and peacefully in the way you would enjoy. Allow Temperance to take over.

Meditation: Do nothing. Think nothing. Allow all thoughts to pass through your mind without stopping. Do not analyze or criticize. When a thought comes, think only, "thinking," and let the words go by. Follow the breath, merely observing.

Visualization: Take a walk down a pathway of your mind, aiming toward the highest good. Visualize a rainbow overhead and follow it to its end. What is there for you? See yourself reaping the rewards at the end of the rainbow.

Astrological Sign: Sagittarius

Foods: Go to the jars of herbs for tea. Ask them to draw your attention toward those that you need. Make yourself the perfect blend for this particular moment.

Synthesis

There is just the right moment for everything. If you find obstruction in your path, back off just a minute. Take time out to allow for an integration of this new information. Your being wants to create perfection, but perfection cannot be forced. If things are not working out well, take a break, especially a mental break. Let go of how you were looking at the situation. Allow the superconscious to do its tempering work of synthesis.

It will then re-inspire you to right and harmonious action. Harmonize. Imagine there is a smooth flowing river of life with a strong current just for carrying you effortlessly forward. Step into it in your mind's eye. Feel the gentle push and let your body float on it. Just a moment's visualization can put you right on course. It gives your higher being time to see what's really needed. It may only be an adjustment of thought, a slight change in plans, but the increment of difference may be all that is needed to make everything happen easily.

15 TRICKSTER

Number and Meaning: 15, Realization of bondage begets liberation

Traditional Name: The Devil

Medicine Woman Energy: Captivated by the Trickster

Affirmation: "The primal Will-to-Heal within me is stronger than any thought, thing, person, disease, habit, or practice that attempts to rule my life. I do now fully realize my power to change all that appears to oppress me."

The Card Speaks: "I am the force given power when one assumes the attitude that the material world rules hir. I am given power when you look only backward to that which *has been* your experience, and when you allow those previous apparent failures to rule your walking. 'Devil' is 'lived' spelled backward. It is living and looking only to what has been. In other words, it is really the opposite of living, which is a moving forward. You are chained by the point of view that what is 'out there' limits you. You can transmute this Devil by realizing that the past can be transcended.

"The sorcerer Don Juan spoke of a 'warrior' as one having no personal history. By this he meant that to be a person of power one must let go of the 'memory' of one's own failures. You must reevaluate. You must re-value. You must live and go forward.

"All that appears to have limited you on the material plane, whether laws or people or situations, must be made into your benefactors by your own mental processes. The Devil then becomes merely the Trickster, causing you to look at yourself and discover where you are caught by the world. You may want to rebel against outside forces that appear to harm you, but the only true revolution is evolution of consciousness. Material experience follows mental experience. 'Black is Beautiful' is the mental construct that changed the consciousness that freed black people from bondage. 'Women's Liberation' encompassed the idea and image of women as a large group (51 percent of the population) worthy of respect and self-love. This concept was the inspiration leading to the actions leading to freedom from oppression.

"The Devil is faulty observation, superficial reasoning that gives physicality more power than spirituality. Remember, the body dies easily, the spirit is infinite. This stage of growth means moving beyond appearances, experiencing beyond the senses. Sexuality is more than sensation. Life is more than the material plane. The Devil dies to life. You have lifted the chains when you understand this.

"As you come to know me as the Trickster, you will discover that I capture your compassion. By leading you into situations where you experience the inequities of the world, you are drawn to change them. As you see that others suffer with you, your heart takes a spiritual step. When you have moved beyond blame, beyond the idea of Devil and the expression of rage at an unfair world, your open heart begins to transform the energy of anger into the action of love. I have tricked you into becoming a compassionate being. Only now are you able truly to help the world. Your heart will reach for the Spirit."

Self-questioning: Whom do I blame when something goes wrong? Do I look to myself? Do I check out my own beliefs to see how they brought the situation to me? Am I called to anger or to action that might make correction?

Exercise: Recall a situation where you felt oppressed by forces outside yourself. List three other possible ways you could have interpreted (valued) the situation. Now consider the results of each way of valuing.

Meditation: Allow an image of someone toward whom you hold a resentment to come to mind. Release this person from your resentment by taking off the chain by which your feeling attempts to bind them. In this way, you forgive them and release yourself at the same time. Place the situation in the hands of a higher power.

Visualization: Think of a situation in your present life where you feel overpowered by the world, victimized by what seems uncontrollable. Allow the knowledge of what you can really do to come to mind. If it doesn't present itself immediately, make up a fantasy of yourself taking power and control over this aspect of your life. See the fantasy through to its successful completion. If you weren't pleased with how you handled it in your first fantasy, begin again, and come up with an alternative method. Do this until you find one that makes you feel good (as opposed to vindicated).

Astrological Sign: Capricorn

Unchained

It is easy to feel trapped, limited by circumstances, poor because no one will give you a job, hungry for lack of a handout, and so on. There seem to be endless restraints on us in the "vale of tears" as life is sometimes called.

Indeed, for all practical purposes, life can be a struggle, full of sorrow and pain. Why is this so? Once again I am drawn to play with the word "evil" and transpose the first two letters, creating "veil." These worldly evils are a veil that hangs over our eyes while our consciousness clings to the belief that it is through material means that our liberation comes.

We struggle to make more money, believing money will wipe out the feeling of poverty. I say "feeling" because the amount of material wealth one is happy with can be far below what is called the "poverty level." We struggle to combat disease at its symptomatic end, rather than to create conditions of health in self and Earth through proper living. We cry for the suffering, hungry victims of societal abuse, but do little to create a new society. We give our days to society's jobs, our children to be taught in their schools the very values whose results we see and abhor. We suffer through relationships that stifle creativity and spirituality, so that we don't have to risk being our greatest Self. Oh, the ills of the world are great indeed, and we love to feel victimized and abused.

But there is another part of us that emerges as we rise above any of these conditions. And from our liberated view we see that we pulled ourselves up by our very own bootstraps, whether from our own determination or the help of God as we allowed it to work through us; and we want to show others the way. This is a big step, a good step, but not the last step.

We must also rise above the struggles of others. It is a blessing to get beyond one's own limitations, but, lo and behold, you are then confronted by an entire world of suffering beings.

Anyone who works in the field of social services knows what a burnout it can be to try to help others by material means. Admittedly, help can be given. Money, food, medicine, and shelter are immediate satisfiers. But the problem is eternal. It can be completely solved only by changes in consciousness, just like the awakenings you made when you realized you could do something for yourself.

This does not mean you must not offer material help if the opportunity is before you. You must follow your conscience. That is your spiritual growth. And as you awaken, your greater spiritual power will have more effect on the world than any good deed you ever did.

It is your love, kindness, and generosity that help the world. Your offerings are simply the material representations of your inner growth. Consequently, you must not seek the material offering to solve your problems, but those spiritual qualities higher than your own. This way, the Trickster is foiled. You are freed. The veil is lifted. The Devil is no more.

16 PIERCED SHIELD

Number and Meaning: 16, Revolution

Traditional Name: The Tower

Medicine Woman Energy: The Shield is Pierced; Thunderbird Rises

Affirmation: "As old structures dissolve, my good evolves. I am filled with new inspiration. False concepts are destroyed as I release that which limits my joy and well-being."

The Card Speaks: "Your shield is the thought structure you have created through living. It is built of words, attitudes, and concepts that, as you instituted and accepted them, served to protect your tender inner being. But there comes a time when old patterns, for your own good, must be broken. I come to destroy that which is no longer useful to you, to down the Tower of Babel, to dismantle false hopes and erroneous assumptions.

"It is time for concepts based on the idea of separation between Self and the universe to be replaced by the knowledge of Self in relation to the whole. Old ego-purposes are revealed and knocked down. There is realization of a greater Cosmic Will working within. It is the end of saying, 'I can't help it, that's just the way I feel.' Subconscious motivations are brought to your awareness. Your present level of consciousness now sees your old level of consciousness's false expectations. These are the lessons I teach.

"The Tower falls so that you may grow. Like a lightning bolt, I clear the air. My light pierces the darkness. The experience of me is one of great intensity. I strike to convert

105

your energy to better current use. I may destroy the old job, relationship, viewpoint, or whatever is in the way of your current potential. As you move through these situations, remember *your good cannot be destroyed.* Only that which is oppressing you is dissolving.

"If you have been making affirmations in order to change your life, you must realize that all that restricted you must be shaken loose. Remember, too, that whether you consciously affirm change or not, every thought affirms a reality. Is it the one you want to reinforce? You constantly create your life through your use of the unseen forces of thought and image. Through the elimination of those concepts that limit your good, your energy is released to serve the whole."

Self-questioning: Am I taking the next step I know is before me?

Exercise: Write a few pages on one of your major turning points. Did you have feelings of separation or polar thoughts before the experience? How were they harmonized afterwards? Was there any literal shakeup at the time, such as an automobile *crash*, or a lightning *storm* or flashing *lights*? Did you *break* things? How was the shield of your belief system pierced?

Meditation: Imagine a tower up a hill from where you begin your meditation. The tower has seven floors, each one with a particular significance. Go to the tower, exploring one floor at a time, and learn what each floor has to tell you about your life.

First floor. This is the Red Room. It will contain things that tell you about your work situation or basic life-support system.

106

Second floor. This is the Orange Room. It will contain things that tell you about your social life, group, and family situations. It may also speak about your general health and sense of well-being.

Third floor. This is the Yellow Room. It will tell you about your personal power and self-expression.

Fourth floor. This is the Green Room. It will tell you about your sense of connection with all that is, your relationship to nature and other life forms. It will speak of higher levels of love in personal relationship.

Fifth floor. This is the Blue Room. It will tell you about your creative energies and may have hints as to how to express them more fully. It may talk to you about your ability to speak out and stand up for what you believe in.

Sixth floor. This is your Darkened Room of Prayer. Leave all of your requests here. Begin to see your life as you would prefer it to be.

Seventh floor. This is the Violet Room. Rest here and allow the violet light gently to cleanse and heal you.

Each room may also speak to you about other things you need to know right now. This speaking could be in the form of words, images, symbolic furnishings, a generalized feeling about the room, fragrances or sounds, or arrangements of furniture and space. Even the textures and line will give a certain message. Trust and learn from this interior tower. Then let it all come to rest in the upper room where the higher portion of your Self can integrate all that you have seen.

Visualization: See yourself building a shield of silvery white light, feel it surround your physical body. You can use it to

107

protect yourself at any time from negative thoughts and forces that others may project your way.

Astrological Sign: Mars

Foods and colors: When everything is upset, eat simply or not at all. Wear the most soothing and comfortable clothes.

The Shield of Beliefs

The beliefs, attitudes, and concepts you hold in your mind are like a shield. They protect you from the dangers you have perceived to be ahead of you. These perceptions of dangers are mental programs which have been given to you by your parents and society to protect you from harm in the created world. However, as you go through life, you may find that some of these beliefs have become more like suits of armor that block your energy flow rather than simply protect.

The Pierced Shield card signifies that you are entering a new realm of experience with your progressing maturity, and you will undergo major perceptual changes. With each major conceptual change, you will automatically create an appropriate new shield. Each shield is a set of beliefs that separates your sensitive inner being from the onslaught of opposing ideas that any belief system encounters.

We live in a world of challenges. Our shields, the belief systems we hold, protect us from being overwhelmed by these challenges. If you had been raised a Christian in the time when Christians were fed to the lions, your conception called "martyrdom" was the shield that protected you from the pain of the experience. Your death was glorified and thereby endurable. If you fought wars for your country, your shield was the idea of freedom for your nation. Your belief made killing tolerable. As a soldier, your belief-shield may have been pierced by an awakening to the experience of suffering by others when you actually confronted it.

Let us say you then devoted your life to peaceful service to humanity. This new belief-shield must now protect you from being overwhelmed by the magnitude of the job. Your new shield, rather than being built of ideas of nationalism, will be made of ideas of humanitarianism.

Humanitarianism will seem like the ultimate shield. Yet, as you grow still further, you may awaken to the idea that not only must you respect all humans, but you must respect all plants and animals as well. Your old shield will be destroyed, often dramatically, and a new one will take its place. Symbolically, the thunderbird will rise. From the ashes of the old belief-shield, a new way of viewing life will form.

Each shield protects for a while and allows you to grow at a certain level of spiritual work. You can see this most easily in others when you try to "raise their consciousness" on certain issues. They can't seem to hear you. Their shield is protecting them from taking steps they are not yet able to take. On the other hand, occasionally you may be the lightning that pierces their shield, shattering their thought constructs for a new awakening.

Just as the sensible warrior would not go to battle without a physical shield, you are not asked to be without your psychic shield. For example, if you are a sensitive, receptive, peaceful Earth healer, you would not be wise to go to a large, crowded city slum and open yourself to requests for help . . . unless you had a very powerful shield of faith and light and perhaps a knowledge of aikido! There are many forms of shields. Rigid, dogmatic ideas are shields. These are often broken down by very rough awakenings. Belief systems that tolerate differences are shields. A simple learning that alternatives exist may be enough to expand these shields. Being very open and receptive can also be a shield when that openness is combined with a way of self-protection, such as imagining being surrounded by a sheath of divine light that filters negativity. Your own psyche may use several kinds of protective shields for different areas of your life.

If you see an area where you are particularly vulnerable, you can create a shield by the following method.

1. Designate the vulnerable area. Let's say it is "loss of relationship." You feel abandoned and helpless when someone leaves you.

2. Identify the feelings that commonly occur. In this case, "abandoned" and "helpless." These are like holes in your shield.

3. Now list five attitudes that might counteract these feelings. Here you would list such things as a sense of belonging to a greater whole, self-confidence, personal power, the ability to take life as it comes, or a sense of adventure.

4. Alongside each of these attitudes, list one thing you already do that stimulates this attitude in yourself and one thing you would enjoy doing that would further build this attitude.

5. Do each of these things more often. The shield is built in practice.

Building your new shield, as you may already be able to see, will not only help you to deal with your vulnerable area, but will develop qualities in you which will tend to make other areas of your life happier as well.

17 THE GRANDFATHERS

Number and Meaning: 17, Ascension

Traditional Name: Star

Medicine Woman Energy: The Grandfathers Who Have Gone before Us

Affirmation: "A light shines forth like a star from the heavens, revealing the wisdom of the ancient ones. I rest on the sturdy foundation of knowledge that comes from a past wholly lived, and I feel supported."

The Card Speaks: "We are a new hope within you. The old patterns of interference have been broken; you have reached a new level of communication with the ancestral energy of Self. As a result, you can now experience renewed health and vitality. Through meditation, you have found your roots, your source of cosmic nourishment.

"We are the Grandfathers. We have walked on the ground upon which you now walk. You are beginning to realize the meaning of our lives and are able to continue in our footsteps. We will begin to teach you of your spiritual heritage, for you carry within you a particular way of walking on the sacred path.

"It is your destiny to carry on from where we have led you. You drink from the waters of Earth and now from those of the heavens as well. You are able to take our highest vision and bring it into reality. You, who have a foot in both worlds, are the only one able to lift the consciousness of the human beings once again to a level of hope. It is you who can build anew. It is you who can walk in beauty within the created world.

"Explore now the beauty of your bare soul, this soul you

have found in your spiritual search. Take time now to concentrate on the relationship of yourself and nature, yourself and God, the Great Spirit Within All. We will help you. We will offer what we have learned, that you might learn from our experiences. Speak with us and we will answer."

Self-questioning: Do I know the struggles of my ancestors? Of what value are they to me?

Exercise: Find out about the people who were native to your area of the country. What was their relationship to the land? What were the expressions of their spirit? How can you honor them?

Meditation: Meditate on a crystal (quartz or geode), a very old part of the Earth. Crystals are great receivers and transmitters of energy. They are communication devices. Hold one in your hand and let it speak to you. Look into it and probe its mysteries. Offer through it your prayer to the Great Spirit and a thanksgiving for the native peoples who first walked your land. Perhaps the Grandfathers will come to you.

Visualization: Look upon a star, seeing a ray of light reaching from it to yourself. Travel on that beam of light to the star. Open all of your physical and spiritual senses to receiving its beauty and energy. Take its light back into yourself when you are finished with your journey and visualize yourself as a shining star or crystal. Light up the whole world of your being.

Astrological Sign: Aquarius

Foods: Try the foods of your ancestors. Check your library and your relatives for information. How do these foods affect your state of mind?

112

The Ancestors

There have been many worlds. Each world has evolved, like a person, through successive stages of development, shedding one body after another until all that remains is light. When you wish upon a star, your thoughts are being projected to ancient beings whose consciousnesses have so brightened that they are no longer in need of embodiment. Each star glows with its development.

The blue jewel of Earth now seeks to shine even brighter by increasing the vibration of itself and its beings. Earth Mother ascends into the heavens by aligning the minds of her humans with other brilliantly glowing planets of love and peace. She asks you to look up, lighten up, put yourself in perspective. Take note of all the lives you have lived and all who have lived before you. Each one has contributed its share to the spark and sparkle of the planetary field.

Allow the learning of those who have mastered life to raise you now. Take the hand of the Wise Ones who lead you to the wisdom of the ages. Their knowledge is all around you.

18 THE GRANDMOTHERS

Number and Meaning: 18, Intuition (Infinity Within)

Traditional Name: Moon

Medicine Woman Energy: The Grandmothers Who Are Wise

Affirmation: "All that ever was or will be is here now within me. My body incorporates the planetary dream and my most personal love into a life grace-filled."

The Card Speaks: "We are the Grandmothers, and the moon is our symbol. We are intuitive knowledge that you feel or sense, knowledge that seems to be within your body. Our teaching is this: trust your body. Your body subtly reacts to everything you present to it and gives you feedback as to whether a particular thing is right for you in that moment. At night, when you sleep and dream, your body goes through experiences that it needs in order to live the life you are attempting to live. Your thoughts lay out the blueprint and your body tells you what to do, moment by moment, through its feeling responses. It lets you know if you have erred in your planning. It gives you peace and joy, if you have planned well.

"Thought and action, will and movement, these are the things that reorganize your body cells. Old cells embodying old ideas die and new cells containing your new ideas are born. You are constantly recreating yourself in your own image. This creative energy is so strong that unless you are using your talents and abilities creatively in the world, you may begin creating excess body in the form of fat, or cancer, or perhaps even an entire new person, a baby. Your imagination gives form to the creative energy. Reflect on it.

"New knowledge gained in the reflective state of meditation is incorporated into your body. Your mental organization becomes your physical organism. We are the Grandmothers who speak in wisdom. Break out of your shell, the old ways of thinking that lock you inside. Pass by your personality's desires and your education as well. Walk between the towers of thought, following the path to the high mountain of spiritual intuition. There is infinite wisdom ahead."

Self-questioning: Do I use my talents and abilities creatively in this world? Do I listen to my intuition? What happens when I do?

Exercise: Chart your body cycles with the moon. Do your moods change with her? Note what your body wants you to do at different times of the month. See if you are more peaceful and attuned if you follow the body's suggestions.

Meditation: Open yourself to receiving the message of a wise old woman. Create a pathway in your mind to the place within you where she dwells. Let her speak.

Visualization: Place your awareness in the very top of your head, and imagine what your hair would be like if it were healthier, shinier. Go on down your face, seeing your eyes very clear, your complexion glowing. Go over every detail of your face and your entire body, inside and out, visualizing every part, step by step, in its healthiest state. Create your own beauty to your own standards. Know that as you do this, you program your subconscious to move you in the direction of actually having such a body. Don't hold back, only the Grandmothers are listening.

Astrological Sign: Pisces

115

Foods and colors: What are the foods and colors that you associate with your Grandmother? Now is the time to try out some of her recipes, perhaps some of her ways. What was the path she trod?

Psychic Birth Control

Your body contains the wisdom of many bodies. Your learning is not just that which you have acquired in this current life. You can tap the expertise acquired by others simply by visualizing them, opening to their particular talents, and seeing the flow of these talents enter into yourself. Your visualization puts you in an energy alignment with the life experiences that will, over time, allow you to become more and more in tune with that on which you focus.

Contemplating God, one likens oneself to God, bringing about the experiences of purification of one's being which draw one to the ultimate enlightenment. On a more mundane level, contemplating peace brings peace; contemplating golf balls brings golf balls (yes, you will notice them more and more!); disease brings disease; love brings love. The manifestation is not often instant, perhaps due only to our short attention span and inability to keep our mind on any one thing. But we do plant seeds with every thought on which we dwell. The longer we allow it to rest on any one thing, the more we are inclined to draw that thing to ourselves.

If you wish to produce a happy marriage, a fulfilling job, a healthy baby, a work of art, or a peaceful world, the process is the same. Put your mind to it. The body will follow. The body contains immense creative resources. It is constantly re-creating itself in your image. Use this force wisely. Dwelling on fears, unwanted possibilities, anxieties, losses, disappointments, and dislikes tends to prolong their life with *your* creative power.

As stated previously, thought power is not usually an instantaneous magical cure. But it will lead you directly to lessons in living that will cause you to learn what you need to know in order to manifest what you are seeking to produce. Think of the mind as a womb. Babies have a gestation period. In that time, the mother goes through a lot of learning. She prepares consciously and unconsciously for what is inevitably ahead. The preparation may not all be sweet. Challenges will occur to the extent that the outcome you are after is alien to your current lifestyle. Just as it would be hard for a mother bear to produce a tiger cub, it would be hard for a shy person living in an isolated village in Australia to become the president of General Motors. Your "baby" is going to be something like yourself. Your product—the manifested outcome of your visualized idea—will be an outgrowth of the kind of person you have been and the life you have led thus far.

If you are just beginning to take over the control of your mind, you cannot expect to manifest instant results of visualized desires that are way out of the range of possibility as you perceive it. Start small and "close to home." Just stretch your limitations a little at first. It's okay to visualize the best possible outcome, but realize that the farther away or more impossible it seems, the longer it is likely to take and the more lessons you may have to learn to get there.

Your psychic power (mind control) can be used for everything from manifesting four dollars to go to a movie to controlling the conception of a child within your body. But you must realize the consequences of your risk. And you must realistically assess the challenges that may come to you as a result of your manifestation process. In the case of the four dollars, if you don't get it, it probably will be only

117

a minor, short-term disappointment. If you do get it, it may be because you caught a glimpse of a want ad that said, "One hour's work needed, four dollars." In the case of psychic control of conception, having a child you don't want could be devastating. On the other hand, if you are willing and able to accept that possibility, you will be led to life experiences that will cause you eventually to be able to exert this much control over your physical/spiritual being.

Using your mind power has many side effects. All of them can be beneficial if you consider the risks you are willing to take as you learn what is needed in order for your life to be revolving (even temporarily) around that which you are attempting to manifest.

The general guidelines for becoming a womb of conscious creation are:

1. Conceive the best possible world for yourself.

2. Become pregnant with ideas that please you and inspire you.

3. Gestate health, wealth, and happiness as you define them.

4. Prepare for that which you hope to manifest.

5. Visualize your creative energy flowing toward what you want to produce. If it is not a baby, then it had better be something else all-involving! You are tapping a powerful core. Be ready to use it.

6. Fill your mind-womb with success stories that turn you on. Somewhere there is a culture and an age that you can strongly identify with if you don't like the one you are in. Go there . . . at least in books and fantasies. Open to the people's wisdom.

7. Look high. Find a Goddess or a Grandmother to serve as a model and midwife to your creative outcome.

8. Act on the impulses that seem to put you closer to your goal. The body is the final processor of your creative mind-baby. It has to do it in the end. Doing is the birth experience itself.

9. Celebrate. You are done. The creation is real. The idea has become flesh. Your spirit is embodied. Relax and enjoy.

You don't have to *get* creative. You already are. You just have to grab the reins of power and take over. Harness your dreams and intuitions and GO! Life will bring you every experience you need to succeed.

19 REBIRTH

Number and Meaning: 19, Early stage of adeptship

Traditional Name: Sun

Medicine Woman Energy: Rebirth of the Living Spirit

Affirmation: I am reborn, a child of Light, aglow with inner vitality. Sun Father, Earth Mother, I am yours. In all things great and small, I see the beauty of your divine expression."

The Card Speaks: "I am the sun. I am the turning toward life that has been made by your individual consciousness. You have shed the old habits of death and destruction through your simple turning of the mind toward me. I am the power of regeneration. I am the turning point. You have freed yourself from the limitations of circumstances. Now, in touch with Creator, you express the one true Self in new creative energy.

"You may find yourself suddenly writing poetry, painting, acting, singing, dancing, or perhaps choosing to bring another being into life. You may begin to feel as though you are a child yourself. You have been born again, and it is only through this experience of me that you enter the eternal land of promise.

"I am the doorway, the bright light at the end of the tunnel. You may enter and pass through me if your heart is filled with wonder, empty of doubts and fears. Like Jesus Christ, the sun/son on earth, you have found the kingdom of God to be within you. This divine Father-light now joins with the Mother-love of your earthly being, creating a heavenly union. Let your heart be light and gay, now that your whole and holy parents have been found. You are the new sun, the Christ consciousness reborn on Earth this day."

Self-questioning: Am I more afraid of the dark or of "The Light?"

Exercise: Soak up the sun. Contemplate its luminosity. Think of it as a being. What does it do for this planet? What would life be without it?

Meditation: Simply dwell on the face of Jesus Christ or any other Master of Light.

Visualization: Imagine that you are walking through a tunnel of darkness heading toward a doorway of light at the end. Do not stop your concentration until you reach the light.

Astrological Sign: The sun

Foods and Colors: Surround yourself with golden oranges and yellows. Eat fresh foods picked at their peak.

Jesus, Avatar

Over the two thousand years since this particular son of God was asked to walk the Earth as human, the popular stories of his life have become very narrow, self-serving legends. One of these legends may have turned you away from the religious path of your childhood. Yet, here you meet again on the inward journey.

Whether or not you were raised Christian, you have no doubt felt the influence of Christianity in your world. Whether you judge the influence of established Christianity to be positive or negative is not the issue being addressed here. Instead, we are looking at how an enlightened being—an avatar or son of God—might live within the realm of the Mother Earth.

Looking at the life of Jesus, you can observe one of the ways a divine soul offers himself as an example of living according to the sacred way that unfolds within him. The avatar may teach or preach, but always he or she lives the way to God. His or her mind rests in the higher kingdoms, not in the worries and fears of the world. The world is dealt with. Day-to-day issues are faced. But the avatar is guided by something more important to hir.

To live as a son or daughter of God, you must raise your thoughts to the level of highest possibility. This might be called "hope." You must transcend doubts by continued action that you judge moment by moment to be in the greater good, seeking no particular reward for your personal being other than that of truly serving the divine. This has been called "faith."

Often faith is misunderstood as some kind of trust that things will turn out as *you* want them. At this level of consciousness, however, your wants have merged with a higher order. You are not so interested in what you get out of something, but rather that the greatest good is happening for all. You are not trusting that God will take care of you, but that God will take care of the great cosmic destiny through you. This is perfect faith. You trust the worth of your small action, if done to the best of your ability, to be a necessary portion of the greater plan. You don't even need to know what the Great Plan is. Acting in faith, you simply assume your acts are a part of it.

You are guided by love, compassion for all life forms, a virtue that used to be called "charity." This guides every avatar's actions constantly. It must guide yours. Before the two thousand years of Jesus's work on Earth is done, everyone living must become an avatar. Everyone must daily live in faith—consciousness of the greater good; hope—affirming the highest possibility; and charity—loving compassionately. Only then will there be rebirth and the liberation of the Mother who has given up her life while her children grow from their two-thousand-year infancy. The son, Jesus, was one of many children who fulfilled her dreams for humanity. Now it is time for all of us to awaken.

You and your brothers and sisters, like Jesus, are children of God. You are daughters and sons of a divine male and female force, and you have come to be foster-mothered by Earth while you grow to spiritual maturity. The greatness of avatars is within you. If you study the life of Jesus or any master teacher who walked the Earth, you will get a sense of the themes of devotion that ran through their beings. You will see that there are many ways to serve God, but all require a cosmic consciousness, a vision of the good of the whole, a constant placing of the personality or ego-self in the position of child to divine father within.

20 DISCERNMENT

Number and Meaning: 20, Initiation

Traditional Name: Judgement

Medicine Woman Energy: The Wisdom to Discern

Affirmation: "I recognize the circle of life brings undeviating justice to all things, events, and beings as all unite in consciousness. I realize my every thought, word, and movement affect all creation. Through time, the great circle returns all things to their maker."

The Card Speaks: "Judgment is simply the return to Self of that which Self has given forth. From the mountaintop, you can look back and see the footprints of your path through the snowy valley of life. Here, your heart can open to all, for you see clearly from on high. No anger is stored. No judgment is hidden. Now, you have learned to express what needs to be expressed, to empty the heart and open its doors for true love to enter.

Judgment symbolizes our resurrection or rising above the illusion of separation. Here we find cooperation not only with people, but with the forces of nature and all life. There is no more sense of being judged or of judging others, as we accept all as a unity of interaction. This is a new plane of awareness.

"At this level of being, you have acquired the capability of discernment. You know your proper place at any given moment and the proper place of others. Your experience has given you the wisdom with which to make decisions that may leave someone out and let another in, but now you do this without judging those people or yourself.

124

Instead, you discern correct action at any given time and you are unafraid to take it. You are able to speak your mind without guilt.

"You may find that you are increasingly sensitive to sound. The vibration of truth is a sound that can be perceived in your own and someone else's words. Now you are sensitized to it.

"From this plane of awareness, your life can be reviewed and all accounts settled. You will know the impact your words have on others. Old events may be perceived in a new light. What was once seen as a hindrance now can be seen for its value in helping the Self to gain certain qualities and experiences necessary for the awakening that has come about. Welcome to the level of consciously working with us, the Guides of humanity."

Self-questioning: Am I capable of expressing what I think without harsh judgment of others?

Exercise: Listen.

Meditation: Spend half an hour chanting *om* aloud. Then be silent for half an hour.

Visualization: See yourself ascending a rainbow stairway to the heavens. Put yourself into that ascending body and begin to feel yourself walking up those stairs. Imagine that you can pierce the clouds and hear the call of celestial music. Reach for the angelic hand outstretched and go where you are led.

Astrological Sign: Pluto

Foods: Every religious tradition has had certain suggestions, if not rules and taboos, on which foods help one to be on the highest spiritual path. Definitely, foods affect the body in very specific ways. If you have been utilizing these lessons fully, you have seen how certain foods affect your own body. You will also discover that when you eat according to a certain diet, your own feelings or "vibes" become different from others who are not eating the way you are.

Religious groups or even families are more in harmony with each other when they partake of the same general diet. Many spiritual teachers eat very lightly, gaining an extra sensitivity to the needs of their people. Adopt the diet of a religious tradition or exalted teacher you respect. Notice the change in your own vibration as you allow yourself to become aware of the diet's effects. Do you gain more understanding into the person or tradition? Do you feel more akin? Learn from this.

Colors: See how real gold or diamonds affect the way you feel. Why are these so valued throughout the world? Can you find their inner worth? What is the stone of your land, its color and place in your life? How do you feel when adorned with jewelry that carries special meaning for you? How do you feel completely unadorned? What are your true colors? Experiment.

Find out when certain colors or stones felt important in your life. During what periods? During which relationships? How did the color help you?

Surround yourself with a color and see what sound it brings to mind. Try listening to different sounds and see what colors they bring to mind.

Toward Discernment

During times of self-reflection, there is an evaluation of the actions of self and others. In the early stages of understanding, you may easily judge others as wrong. "If it weren't for them, I would have been able to. . . . " The best thing to

126

come out of judging others wrong is the desire to be unlike "them" oneself. You vow to remain better or to become better than that which you are perceiving as outside yourself.

As you become more aware of how your thoughts and actions draw events and people to you, you begin to judge situations differently. It is no longer simply "I am totally right and they are totally wrong." You begin to see where "you asked for it" or "played right into their hands." This is the second level of judgment leading toward true discernment. At this stage, you begin to see more clearly where others are misjudging or pre-judging others and you want to help these "prejudiced" and "judgmental" people to see their errors and become more fair. Of course, you are still judging them and may become irritated at your own judgments.

All of this leads to the third stage of judgment. Here we might call it a further refinement of discrimination. You are sorting out that which is beneficial to you and that which is not, but you are no longer making blanket decisions to rule out someone or something merely by its general classification. You are distinguishing between subtleties. In the area where you do this best, you would be considered a connoisseur. Your tastes and perceptions are very refined. This is a high level of the quality of judgment and it is easy to want to stay here. But remaining at this level will become just as distasteful to the spiritual seeker as remaining at either of the first two levels.

The next step in your personal evolution is to go beyond these necessary, developmental stages. The path looks something like this.

Egotistical self-righteousness: I'm always right.

Blind dogmatism: My group is always right.

Prejudice and judgmentalism: My values are better than someone's.

Discrimination: I can tell you to the smallest detail why one thing is better than another.

Discernment: I can see a reason for it all and the part I play in its creation. I can also choose not to play my part.

Discernment is a willingness to look and listen attentively to the information before you, whether that information comes in the form of a person, a creed, an event, or even the simplest of words and actions. You take the time to reflect on the reason for its being placed within your field of awareness. You accept the part you played in drawing it to you. And if you don't like it, you accept your role in dismissing it from you.

As you can see, it is very hard at this level to get too uppity about anything. And at the same time, you can and must make choices. But these choices are based on the refined senses you have developed along the way during the early stages of judgment.

Discernment is a liberation from the roles of either victim or oppressor. You have ascended. You may now trust yourself to carry out the divine will by trusting and acting on what feels right to you in each moment. Your mind, spirit, body, and emotions are a coordinated unit acting with full knowledge of your relationship to the whole. The mind, body, spirit, and emotions now know experientially that what you sow, you will also reap. The circle of life is clear.

21 DANCER

Number and Meaning: 21, Attainment

Traditional Name: The World

Medicine Woman Energy: Dancer in the Winds of Time

Affirmation: "The present is my point of power. All light, all love, all energy, pass through me now creating ongoing beauty, balance, and awakening on the path toward infinite bliss. From death, the pause of perfect peace, I am born to dance on top of the world."

The Card Speaks: "I am Cosmic Consciousness, an awareness in the now of the many forces at work on every plane of existence in and beyond this world. In a sense, I am what has been referred to as the New Age, when all is in balance and everyone lives in peace and harmony recognizing their oneness with each other. I am the end of an old cycle and the beginning of a new one.

"I am a sign that all have learned to work *with* nature, using the laws of nature to the benefit of all. The streams and rivers flow, turning the water wheels; the wind gives its power to the windmills; the sun warms homes and gives light. Each element and being is recognized for its worth and utilized in beneficial ways, according to the Creator's plan.

"You are now a co-creator, taking part in the planetary transformation now taking place. Self and world are one being, breathing one life. You are the Dancer holding wands of male and female life force in perfect balance. The polarities within the self have been recognized and brought into a conscious creative working relationship. There is

129

synthesis, crystallization, perfection, stability, all within the greater flow. You move consciously with the cosmos, understanding your place in time.

"I dance freely and with power, for I have faced the death of all that flows through me. In other words, I have transcended possession and desire for results. My actions are based on the fullness of the moment rather than on sacrifice for the future. I understand that now is all futures. I therefore live in death. It is death as a state of constant peace and surrender to what is. Thus, death is the ultimate balance during life. I have united polarities of existence. As you approach the understanding of this within yourself, the world is yours. In Earth, I *am* through you."

Self-questioning: Moment to moment, I need only ask, "Am I in harmony with the good of all portions of myself?" and to breathe in peace and exhale love. Ask yourself this question ten different times today.

Exercise: Go to a high place and dance with these thoughts in mind.

Meditation: Take your state of peaceful mind into your everyday life and rejoice.

Visualization: Lift off from the world, in your mind's eye, and look down. See this small glowing blue planet. See where the trouble spots are and breathe them light.

Astrological Sign: Saturn

Food, Colors: The world is yours from which to choose.

I will be happy forever
Nothing will hinder me
I walk with beauty before me
I walk with beauty behind me
I walk with beauty above me
I walk with beauty below me
I walk with beauty around me
My words will be beautiful

—from the Navajo Blessingway

Being a Channel of the Divine

The four powers of creation are now freely flowing through you. You fully realize the purpose of each, and now it is for you but to allow them to fulfill that purpose through your own personal life. You know that each action you take, no matter how small, affects the entire world. At the same time, you know that the only choice you ever need to make is to go with that inner flow of harmony you have now learned to sense.

You have the power of all directions at your command. You have taken ideas from inspiration (East), through planning (South), through maturity (West), and through the destruction of your creation into death (North), letting them go and opening to the resurrection of energy as a fresh new idea emerges again from the East. A dancer must let go of one step in order to move on to the next. A musician must release one note to find the next. Rhythm and harmony require constant shifts and balances. This ability to receive, integrate, and let go is what the tarot has been teaching you throughout the Major Arcana, the Great Mystery.

Now you have but to dance your dance of life. You may stumble, fall, and pick yourself up to start again, but you cannot truly err if you trust in your basic being. You are universally connected. There is no way you can be lost forever. No matter how far you might veer from your perfect path, the events of life will bring you back over and over again until you reach that center point of power within yourself, until you reach ultimate confidence in your own thought, word, and deed. The strands of life continually pull you from all directions until you take full command of the reins of power within your being. Then you are not like a puppet on a string, but rather a dancer pulling the strings gracefully as she sways with the winds of time.

The Four Powers

The Minor Arcana: Your Four Powers

The twenty-two Major Arcana are cards depicting the Great Mystery of life and the roles we are asked to play on our road to understanding it. These roles lead to full participation as a co-creator of life on Earth. A person may spend hir entire adult life in one primary role, let us say, for example, the Emperor (Command), learning to take command for the good of the whole. Yet, in any one lifetime, the energy of each other card is experienced, at least for short periods, many times over and over again. The Major Arcana involve you in the Great Mystery of life and teach long-term soul-level lessons.

The Minor Arcana, the Four Powers cards, depict the lesser situations of life, the everyday struggles and pleasures that make life interesting. Each suit deals with one main aspect of your being—body, spirit, mind, emotions—and a symbol for the expression or use of that aspect—Stones, Pipes, Arrows, Bowls—is given to remind you of the essence of each level. Stones remind you that your physical being is of this Earth. Pipes, being hollow reeds, remind you that an energy or spirit flows through your physical body. Arrows remind you that you must direct or aim your mind and thought power. Bowls help you to realize that you are a container of emotion, giving and

The Four Powers

134

receiving.

Seasons and directions are also related to the different suits as shown on the chart "The Minor Arcana: The Four Powers." The cards progress from ace to Exemplar to show the evolution of an idea to its mastery. There are fourteen stages (cards) through which every idea can evolve if it is to be taken to its highest conclusion. Not every idea we receive will we want or be able to take to mastery. But it is helpful to realize when we do choose to move toward successful completion that these steps must be taken. A tarot reading will show you where you are and thus, what you must do next in order to move further toward your accomplishment. How to lay out the cards for a reading will be explained later.

Before doing any readings, it is best to familiarize yourself with each card, perhaps taking one a day and meditating on the image it carries. This is also a way to glean the more subtle psychic energies of the card when you find it showing up in a reading. For best results, always let the card image speak to you in an intuitive way rather than relying totally on the meanings given for the cards in this or any other book. The cards are meant to trigger the workings of your own psyche and are not, in themselves, the final word. As you come up with answers to the questions of your readings, you will begin to know yourself; this is the aim of the tarot. Each card guides you to an inner awakening of the answers hidden inside your own consciousness.

Now, take some time to study the groups of cards (suits) as a whole. See how they relate to each other and to life's challenges and life's rewards.

The Minor Arcana: The Four Powers

	STONES	PIPES	ARROWS	BOWLS
	North Winter Night	East Spring Dawn	South Summer Noon	West Fall Sunset
	Resources	Channels	Aims	Devotions
Ace	Crystalize the idea of prosperity.	Awaken to exciting possibilities.	Will to do.	Receive love from the Giver.
2	Reflect on potential use of resources.	Recognize the call to act.	Aim high above the common thought.	Conceive of love with another.
3	Gather together that which is needed.	Dream, envision, wander.	Listen to your heart.	Enlarge your circle of spiritual kin.
4	Establish basic self-sufficiency.	The discipline of expressing your true nature attracts.	Contemplate your blessings.	Materialize your love into form.
5	Give away the first fruits of your talents.	Allure through opposition or inertia.	Notice the needs the others.	Let go of your gift of love.
6	Restore balance to your accounts.	Accept and receive your blessing.	End struggle; seek higher mind.	Appreciate experiences of the past.
7	Reap a bountiful harvest.	Overcome doubt by action of the self unbound.	Listen to the truths of the sages.	Let the Self be swept into bliss.

The Minor Arcana: The Four Powers

	STONES	PIPES	ARROWS	BOWLS
	North Winter Night	East Spring Dawn	South Summer Noon	West Fall Sunset
	Resources	Channels	Aims	Devotions
8	Develop your craft by continued practice.	Develop your art from stillness.	Commit to a way.	Journey toward the divine in all.
9	Reinvest your energy in the future.	Energize your spirit; soar higher.	Overcome doubt and fear by trusting your decision.	Come home to your spiritual family.
10	Accept recognition.	Return your experience to the world.	Be steadfast of mind.	Celebrate the Goddess in all.
Ap	Expand knowledge of your source and skill.	Feel your body as a channel of power.	Stand by your words.	Devote yourself to joy and peace.
To	Be a keeper of Earth; recycle waste.	Free your mind to fly with the eagle.	See through cultural illusion.	Swim in eternal light.
Lo	Provide plenty.	Radiate energy that empowers.	Liberate by revisioning the world.	Nurture your spiritual family.
Ex	Eternal fertility results.	Your art inspires the future.	Your stories transform the world.	Ever-deepening love welcomes the living spirit to Earth.

Claiming the Four Powers

First of all, you must realize that these Four Powers are ones you were born with and will have all of your life. *No one can ever take them from you*—though sometimes they do try. The more you understand these Four Powers to be totally yours, the less anyone will be able even to attempt to steal them from you or manipulate them through you.

These four energies are basic life forces. You experience them daily. So that you fully realize what they are, I am going to describe them with several different words. You may settle on the words or phrases that best remind you of their power within you.

Stones: The power of Earth or Earth's body; resources; physicality; material things; food; goods; your own body. "From dust (Earth) all things were made, and to dust (Earth) they will return." Everything is made of Earth's elements: wood, metal, air, water, and fire.

Pipes: The power of sex energy; creativity; self-awareness; artistic expression; life force; kundalini; sex drive; sexual expression; spiritual expression; inspiration; excitement; illumination. Your spine is a channel, like a bamboo flute or a hollow reed, through which energy flows. The energy turns the wheels of your life and gives vitality to the events to which you need to respond. Sex and spirituality are intimately connected and the lessons of the Pipes help you understand how this is so.

Arrows: The power of mind; thoughts, concepts, attitudes, beliefs; philosophies of life; concentration; will; attention; contemplation; meditation; organizing and managing; positivity; discipline; wisdom. Whether or not you are consciously in control of your mind power, you are always using it.

Bowls: The power of time to devote to your heart's desire. All you have on Earth is time; what you devote your time to is your choice. Your choice depends on many factors. But whatever you are spending your time doing, you can devote yourself to it. You can, in other words, be devoted. You can love in and through each moment. Devotion is love through time. Time is a receptacle for your love. Thus, you may describe this power with the word you most need to focus on: love, devotion, time, commitment, relationship, fulfillment, enrichment, attunement, offering, spiritual practice, at-one-ment, family caring, hearts, healing actions, karma yoga, service, love in action.

As you can see, there are many ways to describe the Four Powers. The important thing to remember is that they are innate within your being. You are embodied. An energy flows through you. You have a mind. And you are able to spend time devoting your life to something. These are the essences of the powers. They make up the Minor Arcana or mysteries of life. The Major Arcana are characters or forces that lead you higher and higher through each "minor" experience, helping you to live life more and more fully, more and more spiritually.

Threats to Your Powers

Let's get the worst out of the way. It is true that someone could take your life, abuse you sexually, give you a lobotomy or make you a slave. These are the vilest of evils we can imagine. Every religion has strict taboos against acts that severely violate the personal space and consciousness of another human being. Yet we have seen gross failures to adhere to these common principles. How do these failures come about? How can you protect yourself from such abuses?

Both questions have the same answer. The way is cleared. To tolerate small abuses clears the way for greater abuses to occur. On the other hand, at any point, to grab the reins of power and begin to make your stand clears the way only for more of that power to manifest through you.

In the Christian tradition, there are what are known as "The Seven Deadly Sins." Reinterpreted to fit our current word usage, the sins are as follows.

1. Rape. Traditionally, this was called "lust," but our current understanding of the essence of this sin is simply to want without regard to the wants of another. In modern language, this is rape. It is the death of respect for another and eventually for oneself.

2. Greed. This means taking without giving anything in return or without regard to consequences. It is the death of generosity and cooperation.

3. Over-consumption. The traditional word for this poison is gluttony. We have come to identify that word with food, but in our industrial/technological consumer society, food is but one of the things over-consumed. The sin is in taking all resources and leaving none for future generations. It is the death of the planet.

4. Arrogance or Pride. Now "pride" has a positive meaning in our language, but the sin to which it once referred was superiority and prejudice, the feeling that "I deserve everything and you deserve nothing." It is the death of civil liberty and peace.

5. Envy or Covetousness. This is a desire for what others possess while feeling a resentment that they possess it and you don't. It is directing negativity toward those who appear happier and better off than oneself. It is the death of self-motivation and growth.

6. Sloth or Powerlessness. Though in today's frantic world idleness may be considered a virtue, the sin that these words tried to point out was that of not taking care of one's own basic needs. It is the idea that you should give to me so I don't have to work to get what I need. It is the death of personal responsibility. It is a complete lack of will or personal power. It is the consciousness of victim, the sufferer. It is the death of the power of "I will."

7. Murder or Avarice. This is not simply killing, for we kill each time we swat a mosquito or weed the garden or use a tree to build a house. It is killing out of spite, hate, greed, gluttony, lust or envy. It is the slaughter of the scapegoat for one's own deadly habits. It is the projection and attempt to kill the shadow of one's own failings. It is the death of the life form. It is the extinction of the species.

I have used the word "sin" several times. It is a harsh word. You can read it instead as "poison" or "deadly action" or "toxic waste" of one's life energy. Any way you read it, it spells the worst of what is. These poisons are the waste you are trying to weed out of your system or the societal system in general by your study of spiritual matters. Don't be afraid to look at the illness in order to heal it.

Often aspirants to the spiritual path do not like the concept of sin and do not like to look at the negative side of things. Yet every spiritual system asks us to move away from these Seven Deadly Actions: rape, greed, over-consumption, arrogance, envy, powerlessness, and murder. Though systems differ as to how to rise above these ways of being, they agree that there are virtues to engage in that will help you transcend the sins. The tarot is one system of transcendence. It seeks to uplift every aspect of your life through image and prayer so that the seven deadly actions are never able to be committed against you, nor are you ever desirous of committing these acts of death upon your

141

world and its beings.

To counteract the forces that lead to these deadly actions, you must keep a balance in your own life and contribute to a balanced culture and world society. The balance is between giving and receiving, planting and harvesting, taking from the Earth and giving back to her. The balance is between self and others, inner work and outer expression, feast and fast, silence and speaking out, work and play, sexual freedom and self-respect, creative outpouring and time for inspiration, thought and emptiness, time to seek God and time to allow God's manifestation. It is not a balance of equal amounts of good and evil.

The forces that lead to the Seven Deadly Actions are those that thwart the expression of your Four Powers. Any obstacle to the fulfillment of one of these four circles of power is a force of death, a force of darkness. You can overcome any force of darkness, sin, or death by reaffirming your power in the four directions.

North   Renew your commitment to Earth's constant replenishment.

East   Channel your sexual and creative energy toward the expression of the qualities of God: love, beauty, humor, grace, art, and play.

South   Take charge of your thoughts, supplying positive images and concepts wherever you find fear and doubt.

West   Devote more time to acts of love with no strings attached.

These are your four instantly available powers. They

require only the simplest of actions, but create the strongest shields. You will protect yourself from all negative energy and cease to produce negative karma for this life and lives to come. You will enter the four sacred hoops of a life filled with meaning. You will have stepped foot on the path of good medicine.

Stones

The suit of Stones in other decks has been called pentacles or coins. In the original *Medicine Woman Inner Guidebook*, it was called beads. But it has been renamed Stones in order to bring your awareness back to the source of all goods and means of exchange, Earth herself. The substance earth is the raw material for everything made on this planet, including its life forms, the plants, animals, and human beings.

In twentieth-century technological societies, there is little awareness of the consciousness that dwells within anything made of Earth, other than the human form. However, the native peoples of the world have always seen consciousness indwelling all things. It may be easy for you to recognize consciousness in animals, even plants, but what about dirt itself, stones, and human-created goods?

To get a sense of how consciousness might be in everything, try to think of it this way. Imagine the original native people living their harmonious lives close to nature. They lived, acquired wisdom through experiences, and died. Generation after generation was buried in the Earth where bodies were transformed into elemental Earth forms once again. Dust to dust. Bones and flesh changed into smaller and smaller living organisms, microbiological and chemical life elements, the nutrients that create future bodies through the plants, soil, and stones.

Though the soul of the human being has left its material form and expanded into higher levels of life, it has left something of its wisdom in each element from which it had previously taken human form. Literally, the stones are our ancestors. The spirits of our ancestors may live elsewhere in higher vibratory bodies, possibly finished with Earth incarnations, but they have left us their life wisdoms in the substance of earth itself.

How do we discover these wisdoms hidden within things? Natural objects such as plants and stones can be related to in a way similar to how you would relate to human beings. After all, they once were some body. Now their elements have entered a new kingdom, their aliveness and growth have begun following different laws. Their guides are nature spirits and devas, beings mostly unseen by human eyes. Fairies, elves, gnomes, and all of the little people who inhabit Earth Mother's mystery are their friends. If you are among the fortunate few, you may be able to cross from your human spiritual world into theirs through the opening you create by your belief in their existence. But whether or not you see fairies, elves, and such, you can still honor the life you do see, the plants, trees, and stones of Earth's body.

Think of crystals and gems as the crystallization of the purest consciousnesses bequeathed to us by our ancestors. You might think of crystal as Christ-all, a stone created by a Christed consciousness, a clear consciousness of total love. Holding this view, these stones are very sacred. But who can tap this consciousness from the stone? Only those seeking that Christ Light within themselves.

Each gem and stone is an individual entity with a lesson of its own to teach. And each one is also a jewel in the conscious living body of Mother Earth herself. Mother Earth is a very luxurious being, though she may appear quite simple on the surface. Her treasures, like your own, are within. They take some digging and polishing to uncover.

She also has gifts of gold and silver to give you, precious metals, ores, oils, and woods. Most often we receive these gifts, in our modern lives, after they have been manufactured into products by others. It is easy for us to forget Earth's part in their creation. And it is particularly easy to forget the aliveness of these things. Native people once understood that for every process they put a natural object through, they must make up for its loss of aliveness or consciousness by replacing it with their own. Put simply, when they polished and shaped a stone, changing its former integrity, they added their loving desire to create according to an inspired vision. In other words, they put their spirit into each object.

Today we think of artists and craftspeople doing this. But in native lives, every process was art. A builder talked to the trees and stones requesting them to give up their forms to become a dwelling. With their agreement, she would proceed, adding hir love every step of the way. The finished product was then a living thing, a dwelling filled with life energy. You can intuitively sense this energy in any handcrafted item.

What about present-day mass-produced items? These are, for the most part, dead. They have often been taken, no doubt without asking permission from the Earth, as raw materials in a disgraceful and ungrateful way. Nothing has been given back to Earth in return for her treasures, her body laid bare, unloved, unrespected. The materials are handled by a series of unhappy, underpaid, uninspired workers ignorant of their role in this crime. More humans who are also suffering from this disrespect and feel the lack it causes in their lives, try to make up for it by charging a lot of money to replace the worth that has been stolen.

You, simply needing a tool or wanting a tiny pleasure, purchase the goods. Then you become a part of this chain. You have traded your work-earned money for a pretty and useful-but-dead thing. From you, it will ask for life.

If you value it, love it, care for it, use it fully for its purpose, and thank the elements from which it is made, you will have given back the consciousness it was lacking. Ideally, you will then pass it on, an antique shining with the patina of having aged with care. Or you will bury it once again to become the body of Earth Mother, restoring it to its original source.

You may have and enjoy all of the gold and riches of the Earth. You may acquire as many possessions as you wish. Your power, and theirs, comes only from loving them and using them with your own high consciousness. Any object can empower you if you treat it as an entity with whom you have a relationship. Any object can steal your life energy if you are unaware of its life process. If it was not taken from Earth and created respectfully, you must understand that it will haunt you with its desperate need.

Foods are gifts from Mother Earth, too. It is perhaps easiest here to see that you end up healthier if you garden, cook, and eat simply and with love. If you eat highly processed, chemicalized foods from abused soils, your body must simply give up its life force to them. Youth has an abundance of life force and the results of a sugar, soft drink, abused animal, pesticided vegetable diet can go unnoticed for years. But balance will come, either through human awareness and change or disintegration of the body causing death and transformation back into those simple living organisms that create nutrients for Earth. Dust to dust. You must see the circle of life. There is absolutely no taking without giving.

I have elaborated on the suit of Stones because we live in a very material-consuming society and do not see our part in the process. The current technological culture doesn't want to recognize death, decay, disintegration, and transformation. Every precaution is taken against seeing or talking about "the end" because the end is not seen to be also the beginning. But it is. All forms change into new forms, age becoming youth, death becoming life, disease becoming health, goods becoming Earth, Earth becoming us.

There can be no true hoarding of anything. You can only "have" as long as you care for. Loving care of anything— your body, your relationships, your house, your car, your toothbrush, your talent—is all that keeps it going. Leave anything alone without your consciousness maintaining it and it will soon be gone, changed into something else.

To have, you must hold. Hold gently and kindly in your mind the image of loving respect for all beings and all things. Then they will live for you and give life to you as well.

ACE OF STONES: Seed of Prosperity

Ace of Stones

Prayer: Great Spirit, I accept your offering. I am thankful for these material gifts you place before me so abundantly. Mother Earth provides all that I need. The gifts of my ancestors lie within her arms. Your crystal of inspiration calls me to create from the wealth that surrounds me.

Lesson: The Grandmothers and Grandfathers have given their life and consciousness to Earth for us. This is why the mountains and plains are sacred. The native people *are* the land. Others died that we may live. The Earth is alive with their consciousness.

Earth has embodied every God and Goddess who walked the planet. She has received into hir body every prophet and savior, every amazon and warrior, every seer and simple peasant. She is rich with resources.

She says now, "Open your eyes and receive the gift of true understanding from which abundance comes." Prosperity is formed of right relationship to Earth. Open yourself to becoming aware of the wealth of resources surrounding you. Life is everywhere at your command.

If you are currently experiencing lack or burden in the material realm, do the following.

1. Look at your possessions. As you observe each one, ask yourself, "Do I feel thankful for this?"

2. Immediately get rid of everything for which you are not thankful. Pass it on to someone who will be glad to receive it or give it back to Earth.

3. Observe your feelings. Have they changed? Do you still need something? If not, the problem is solved.

4. If you still need something, visualize the thing you desire. Imagine yourself through the whole cycle of appreciating the earthly elements from which it is made, seeing it carefully created, receiving it gladly, giving something you value in return for it, using it fully, and returning it to Earth or passing it on.

5. Relax. The seed has been planted and will grow. You have given it life.

TWO OF STONES: Reflecting on Potential Use of Resources

Two of Stones

Prayer: The fertile ground of nature surrounds me now, waiting with her gifts for me to notice. The Great Spirit within stands ready in my soul to activate whatever abilities I choose. Which will it be? What can I offer to the world that will bring my earthly reward and soothe my soul? I reflect now on myself and where I am. What can I do for this land around me? What can I do for my people? As I activate myself in a chosen direction, the road to prosperity is cleared.

Lesson: You are in a relationship to material things. Think of this as you would a relationship to a friend. Is it a good one? Are you offering your true self or just giving at the surface level? What does the world want from you in relation to what you have to offer?

What attracts you to the world? Which of Earth's things excite you? Do you like to play with her, sing to her, achieve results with her, make things together? Are you at home in nature? Do you like adding your life to the city's?

Now is your time to form a mutually beneficial relationship with the things around you. Think of the world as your lover. What do you want from hir? What are you willing to give?

If you are feeling out of balance, as if you are giving more than you are receiving, you are probably giving surface abilities rather than your true talents. You may be in the wrong occupation. Or you may just be timid in expressing and following your real interests. This will have to change.

149

If you are feeling like you receive too much money, time, or things, there is probably a block in your distribution system. Do the exercise under ace of Stones. Plant your money, time, or goods in the care of some person or organization that really would use them to enhance life on Earth. Do it now.

Your success is the crystal-clear thought of your desire placed into Earth's raw materials. Together you will form the things you both need for a long, happy life.

Three of Stones

THREE OF STONES: Gathering Together

Prayer: Now that I see my potential, I am gathering the tools, materials, and people, and the place in which I can work with them to actualize my goal. I have a beginning plan and I am presenting it. I am assembling whatever will help me to create my goods. I give thanks to Earth Mother for wood and clay and water and fire and metal and stone from which all things are created. The forces are with me now.

Lesson: Gather together everything you have that would help you create the material thing on which you are currently focusing. Think of the people who are empowered to assist you. These would be people who have done it before, people who produce the resources you need, people who utilize the services, or people who are always verbally and emotionally supportive of endeavors such as yours. They would not necessarily be relatives and friends. At this stage, never share with a skeptic an idea you have

150

chosen to manifest.

Look at your skills and see what step of the manifestation you can immediately perform. Do it now. You can increase knowledge as you go. If schooling is required, be sure you have time to continually manifest a part of your dream *as you go.*

You have what it takes to manifest everything you want and need. But your energy and resources must have a clear path opened in yourself before the road will open before you in the material world.

Do what you can do *now* enthusiastically. In time, your energy will draw to you everything else needed. Trust in yourself and go forward. You are at the blueprint stage of success. Be meticulous in your plan. Gather assistance.

FOUR OF STONES: Basic Survival

Four of Stones

Prayer: In the beginning, there are many challenges. The pattern of my design is untested. My product is not yet perfected. I am tempted to give up. Instead, I hold on tightly to the first vision that inspired me to begin. I keep my money in check, not spending too freely, holding the reins. I keep waste to a minimum, finding uses for what I thought would be thrown away. And I continue to build, to mold and shape, until I am pleased with my results. Then, I shall give it all in a spirit of good will.

Lesson: New ventures are risky. Make a list of the three objects you cannot live without. Make sure you have them. If you cannot acquire these free and clear within one week's

151

time, your list may be too technologically complex. Simplify. This is basic survival. Food, clothing, shelter. It may be housing at Mom's or a leaf hut in the woods or finding the house that is within your means. It might mean a supply of grains, learning to fast, or just learning to cook for yourself. It may mean a good warm jacket or postponing a fashion splurge. People are at different levels in maintaining a sense of physical security and comfort. Assess where you are. Arrange everything so that you can, within one week's budget and time limitations, set up a simple life you could fall back on if you lost everything.

Now, having that accomplished, you are ready to risk everything else while you put your new plan into operation. You can proceed worry-free, since you know no matter what happens you will not be left out in the cold. This gives your consciousness the open door it needs to move into your new reality. You have the edge of confidence because you have already provided for your own well-being.

If you are already materially fortunate, this period may be calling on you just to budget wisely. Know what possessions are truly important for your sense of well-being and keep the account that pays for them steady. With everything else you have, energize your plan. This sense of security will free your mind for its creative pursuits.

FIVE OF STONES:
The Giveaway

Five of Stones

Prayer: I shall love my work enough that it is fulfilling in itself. Though I have paid a price and can rightly ask others to pay a price for what I offer, I will give away some of my work simply because I have loved it and for love it can be given. I abide by the spiritual law of tithing: ten percent of my bounty belongs to my people. I give not in order to receive, but because I have already received. Mother Earth blesses me every day with the elements of true happiness. Earth, wind, sky, trees, flowers, the song of birds, and the foods that nourish me are but a few of her gifts. In her name, I return my wares to others.

Lesson: It may seem as though you have lost something. Your situation has changed and some of your assets are gone. But remember, you took this risk when you were at the four of Stones, Basic Survival. Did you dip into your security stash and sacrifice your own well-being to serve someone else's will? Did you hold back your talents, abilities, or true convictions from the material with which you were working?

Don't get attached to this temporary poverty role by adopting a "poor me" attitude. Re-evaluate your position. Take stock of your current resources and review the lessons of the Stones up through this card. It is time to exert mental discipline. Appreciate yourself. Practice contentment with what is. Re-image your future. And relax into the wealth you already have. Change is near.

The Giveaway can be a totally positive experience if you

have provided for your own well-being, put your heart and soul into your work for the sake of itself rather than for reward, and are willing to give your first efforts away to someone you love. This is the spiritual level this card is asking you to reach.

SIX OF STONES:
Restoring Balance

Six of Stones

Prayer: As I am steward of wealth, I am also guardian of the balance of wealth and must share where sharing seems right. I cannot forget the hard times that I have experienced and the help that came to me when I needed it most.

I, too, will give to others whom I perceive to be in need of what I offer. As I teach my skills and share my creations, an inner balance is felt and I am at peace. Wealth comes my way as I embody ideas from the Creator on how to bring peace and comfort to the world. I am asked to create beauty, to support love, to actualize the truth that all are worthy of my care. My response-ability is the power that replenishes the world. Accept these gifts I offer to others, for in so doing, I offer them to you, Earth Mother.

Lesson: You have achieved a level of material success. You must replenish the source. Look back to all those who helped you: family, friends, suppliers, distributors, coworkers and Mother Earth herself. Share something with them. Let your intuition guide you.

SEVEN OF STONES:
Bountiful Harvest

Seven of Stones

Prayer: The seeds I long ago planted have reached their peak. The fruits of my labors are here at hand. Success in my garden comes from working with nature, providing for the lives of the small beings as I provide for the life of myself. I gratefully receive my bounty now.

Lesson: You reap what you have sown in the immediate past. In other words, this current reward has not so much to do with lifetime karma (as would be indicated by the Major Arcana card 10 Harvest) as it does the choices immediately preceding the situation.

Look back at what you have done right and do it again. Your current harvest, promotion, profit, or raise can be repeated. Let yourself feel the pleasure you deserve right now. Take time to enjoy. You should be seeing an outward sign of the inner achievement you feel. If it is hard to see, then make yourself a visible talisman representing this new level of functioning. It will remind you of your power and serve to empower you during future challenges.

EIGHT OF STONES: Crafting

Eight of Stones

Prayer: Nothing pleases me more than to take the elements necessary for my creations and put them together in a way that calls out, "I am beautiful." In my work, I uplift the vibration of the world. Many are pleased and find my goods useful. I make things of quality; I make things strong. I make things fine enough to be loved a lifetime and cherished by all who are privileged to hold them. With the Creator I work as a quality craftsperson. I honor Mother Earth in all I do.

Lesson: You are entering a period of refining your craft. To some, this is not as exciting as the ups and downs of start up or completion. It is the day-to-day routine of pursuing spiritual qualities and making them visible in your work. The true artisan continues to take hir craft to higher dimensions of quality and beauty.

Do not depend on monetary reward to motivate you at this time. Your higher self-expression must be your guiding force. Practice makes perfect. Continue in your present work, improving day to day. Your perseverance will take you to excellence.

NINE OF STONES:
Passing on Knowledge

Nine of Stones

Prayer: Now that I have perfected my product, I am able to share my way with another who aspires to meet my quality. In teaching, I open the way to be filled once again by new and fresh ideas. I continue to grow as I give my old knowledge away. In managing, I am vigilant and clear, yet always kind and gentle with my instruction. Like a loving father, I guide. Like a conscious mother, I provide.

Lesson: Your skills are freely flowing now. Whether or not you have recognition by the world, you can see your success. Your work has brought you many things. You are in greater harmony with the material world and it shows.

Can you handle your changing image? Do you mind the appearance of wealth? You are reaching material maturity. You may be in a parenting or teaching role soon if you aren't already. Mother Earth will be asking you to pass on your knowledge. It is a good time to start someone on your path.

TEN OF STONES:
Accepting Recognition

Ten of Stones

Prayer: My rewards are many at this phase of my career. A good harvest is always certain. People honor me with their purchases. I have earned what I receive. I can relax for a time and rest before I am asked to go on to yet another level of experiencing this work. I can pass some of my wealth on to those behind me and free myself for other things I have begun to desire. It is a rich time in many ways, and greater freedom is coming.

Lesson: You have been "discovered." A place has been made for you in the marketplace. You have found your niche. This can be an exciting and adventurous period. You may at times long for the quiet role of the student or novice. Fame may tempt you to overwork and overproduce.

Use caution. Remember your real values. Keep your priorities straight. Your inner peace and conviction are what brought you here; don't be tempted to set them aside.

You have reached a peak. Always understand that peaks are temporary. Enjoy it. Use it to your advantage. And comfortably prepare for the next phase, which will place you in the role of student once again. You will be moving on to a higher level of learning as an Apprentice of Stones.

APPRENTICE OF STONES:
Expansion of Knowledge

Apprentice of Stones

Prayer: I have heard the creatures of Earth calling. I have heard the sounds of the winds and felt the sun. I have listened to the whisper of trees and seen colors wink and light my way. I am attuned to Earth and heed her call. Now, I can tell others. I can show the way to be quiet and tune in to what is being said across the planet as I walk, to the cries of the dying and the birthing joy of a new day to come. I am a herald of the dawn. I have prepared the Earth for renewal. The Great Mother continues to guide my way.

Lesson: A person of higher status will take you under their wing. You are being led to one who will be a teacher of greater values or broader conceptions in regard to your relationship with the material world.

Hidden powers of your materials may reveal themselves to you. You will begin to see how your work relates to the world as a whole and to the great cycle of life. Spend as much time as you can just attuning to the Earth elements that make up your resources. Look deeply at the original idea underlying your work. See how the Spirit flows through you and through what you do in the world.

Seek deeper sources of wisdom in regard to your craft. Life is an art, and your partner in this project is Earth. How can you make your business together something that produces resources for future generations? You are being asked to grow and expand, to see that as you work the Earth works through you.

TOTEM OF STONES:
Snake, the Crawlers

Totem of Stones

SNAKE
THE CRAWLERS

Prayer: Though my trade may seem humble to many, I am skilled in inner ways. My job may not appear to change the world, but in my consciousness, every movement of my hand corrects a wrong. If I turn a potter's wheel, I turn the Earth and visualize the healing of this planet. If I swing a hammer, I nail a thought of God to someone's house and bestow blessings on each room. When I plant a tree, I put in the hole my power, to grow beneath it, making it strong and making me free. I look like your ordinary worker, but I am learning a higher trade. I am in the school of sacred studies and all life is a lesson to me. Mother Earth is my professor, Father Sun, my guide. My work I do for these who sustain me. Humbly, I carry on through the density of Earth's materiality. Mater, Mother, Matter, you are the expression of all love embodied.

Lesson: You are a keeper of the planet. Study the creatures that crawl the Earth, turning dirt into soil, composting waste. The smallest life forms, the tiniest crawlers, are necessary to break down the larger forms that are no longer needed. Disintegration, death, and transformation are part of the cycle of life.

The snake has always been the symbol of eternal energy and transformation. Healing comes by destruction and rebirth. The old skin is shed and a new one is ready. Life continues. Learn from the creatures who live in Earth's body. They are the humble and the great.

HARVEST LODGE
OF THE STONES:
Plenty for All

Prayer: The more I have cared for the Earth, the more the Earth has given to me. I am wealthy and live in the paradise of my own creation. All that I have ever wanted is here now, a part of me. I have loved Earth's beauty and cast my love upon her. The greatest of my dreams can now be seen in Earth's form. I shall enjoy this, the best of times, and release all guilt from success. This is the moment I have long awaited. The Great Mother and I are one.

Lesson: Great Mother's womb is filled with plenty. The future looks secure. You have stored what is needed and passed on your wisdom. You have replenished the source of your supply. You will be well-fed.

Look to your house of wares. For everything you have gained, have you given its seed to future generations? You are now in charge of the whole system. It must work well beyond your earthly life. Who will carry on and how? Has your blueprint been clearly laid that others may follow?

You may want to note the history of your success for those who come behind you searching. The hungry will be fed by what you leave for them. What do you bequeath to your children? What is the lifeway you leave them?

EXEMPLAR OF STONES:
The Earth Is Eternally Fertile

Exemplar of Stones

Prayer: I have lived well. I have learned of power and wealth. I understand the source of all of these to be but one Great Spirit who breathes life into every living thing. The source of receiving is giving. The source of love is loving. The source of a bountiful harvest is planting the seeds. These words I pass on so that you may be as me. Live fully, for life is a blessing. Love wholly, for love is holy. You can have everything if you are true to that which is really you. Finding your Self and expressing your Self is all that we are sent to do. This is my learning, the lessons of the Stones. This is the wisdom I pass on to you. May all Earth's blessings be upon you.

Lesson: From where you sit, the view is a paradise of everlasting fertility. There is plenty for all. Now is your opportunity to be supremely generous and to teach why you can be. You may pass on the lessons of the Stones.

If you had not cared for life, for things, and for the source of things, you would not be here in this position. Be clear as to how you got here so that others know there is no short cut. Earth Mother is bountiful by nature, but we must work according to her principles.

You now have health only if you have formed a balanced relationship to food and to the material resources you have used as goods to serve your purposes. There is no need to work harder or longer. You understand the cycles and sources of life.

This is the maturity of your Earth cycle. Spend as much

time as possible deepening your understanding of renew-able energy, recycling resources, reincarnation, rejuvena-tion, and reaching optimum physical vitality. Look at aging as Autumn's glory and Winter's sleep. Whatever you put into the body now prepares it for its next life.

If you have keenly observed Earth, you see she will bear again in Spring and so will you. Your Spring soil will be as rich as you have become inside. Your new life will blossom from the old. Remember, death is constantly occurring. Every seven years, each cell in your entire body has been replaced. They are replaced as healthy as the life you live.

The ancestors are alive within us. Their bodies have become the stones, the soil, the plants, our food, our selves. We shall become our grandchildren. We are the future. And we shall live again in the future we are creating now. Contemplate this magnificent cycle.

Pipes

The suit of Pipes is known also as wands or rods in other decks. These are instruments of conduction. The suit of Pipes depicts the energy that flows through you as breath, life force, sexuality, and creativity. Whereas Stones speak of solid things, work, and continuous distribution of re-sources, Pipes speak more of airy processes like imagina-tion, inspiration, and artistic expression of self and spirit.

Life flows through you, stimulating desire, passion, ex-perience of beauty, flowering, and fulfillment. Here you learn to play, to master instruments that bring Spirit to life, including the final mastery of yourself as an instrument of divine grace and power.

The culmination of Pipes energy is the passing on of something of lasting quality. This could be a work of art, a child, or a work of a lifetime. Perhaps it will be all of the above. In the suit of Pipes, you learn to channel inspired energy through your body into creations of a material nature. As you move around the Medicine Wheel into the Bowls quadrant, you will learn just the opposite, to spiritualize the material. With Pipes, you are materializing the spiritual. They are opposite but complementary energies on the Wheel of Life.

In the Medicine Woman Tarot system, Stones and Arrows are opposite each other as well. You can think of Stones as teaching you to recognize and gather resources, and Arrows as doing with resources something that furthers your direction—the direction of Spirit as it flows through your particular life. Each suit or energy is a part of a whole, a part of a great balance that must be kept. One energy is not better than another. Each has its own circle that must be completed within itself, and this is what the cards of each suit show you how to accomplish. Each suit is a wheel within a greater wheel. As each lesson or series of fourteen lessons ends, another lesson or series begins. The circles are ever entwining and spiralling upward.

The energy of the Pipes spirals from the base of your spine up through the top of your head and back down again. Your body is a pipe, stem and bowl—male and female, uniting in the spiritual smoke that rises up to the Creator. Whether you use a peace pipe or a panpipe as your symbol of this energy, a flute or a magic wand, your symbol will remind you to breathe in life and breathe out creation. Your body, as you learn to purify it and use it consciously, will become a better and better conductor of this life force. Eventually, it will be a magic wand itself, a powerful tool for your own transformation and that of the world.

ACE OF PIPES:
Inspiration and Excitement

Ace of Pipes

Prayer: Great Spirit, I am ready. Great Spirit, I open my day with a prayer to you. I look to the East, to the rising sun, and I seek direction. It is Springtime in my heart and I am ready. I listen for your call and ready myself to receive the wand of power. Ignite in me the energy of creation. Inspire a life divine. Awaken in me all possibility.

Lesson: Awaken to inner resources. The magic wand of creative/sexual energy is stirring. This is the kindling of desire. Depending on the level at which your consciousness resides, you are feeling one of the following: a strong need for personal space; increased awareness of your own body; a deep drawing toward family or friends and a desire to be a part of a group that needs you; extra energy to express yourself; an overwhelming desire to do something useful and beneficial for the world; an urge to speak out, sing, or otherwise be heard; artistic inspiration; or an increased longing to merge with God. You may feel more than one of the above.

Puberty and menopause are two times in your life when the creative sexual energy column in your body is filled with excess energy. At these times, the universe gives you a boost of power to get on with your particular forms of self-expression. At other times, you must work spiritually to open to such energy gifts. You must open to love, inspiration, or higher consciousness. At these times, you are suddenly compelled to express, and you feel the freedom to do so. Your appetite is being whetted for a finer level of experience than you have ever had before.

You are filling the pipe with fuel, the force that will eventually alter your consciousness. The pipes of Pan are calling you to the hidden nature of your Self. The morning sun is dawning in your consciousness, calling you into the process of illumination. This is a new beginning for you, a new opportunity. Don't be afraid of its initial wildness.

TWO OF PIPES:
Recognize the Call

Prayer: Great Spirit, I see many possibilities. You have given me a world that is full. Let me know what you would wish from me this day, what work my life may accomplish. I am setting aside things of distraction, that I might hear your words and receive your vision. Guide me along the way that will accomplish your goals. Lead me into relationship with all who will illumine my way.

Lesson: The world is within. As the sacred pipe is lit, your inner vision begins to manifest in the world. The pipe is your spinal energy column where male (the stem) and female (the bowl) unite. The smoke, like male-female flow within your body, spirals around, rising to the Spirit. The eagle, highest flying bird, ascends to give you an overview of a possible life. Fly with it. Look from above.

You are catching a glimpse of creative, sexual, and spiritual possibilities. Right now you are being given a general view. Focus and concentration, zeroing in on one aspect, will come later. You are being magnetically drawn toward fulfillment. This could be a period of excitement and anticipation, accompanying a feeling of readiness.

A possible pitfall at this stage is the tendency to trade your creative/sexual/spiritual energy for money, acceptance by another, or to set it aside for a philosophy. In other words, there is a possibility for self-denial. Instead, you must recognize your potential and seek only to find ways to unite it successfully with the powers of others and the world. The more you dwell on your highest vision, the more you will counteract this tendency toward self-denial and draw support toward yourself.

Three of Pipes

THREE OF PIPES:
Dream, Envision, Wander

Prayer: Guiding ones who come to me in Spirit, I am thankful for your presence. Help me now to see that which I can use to accomplish Great Spirit's work here within Mother Earth's embrace. I am thankful for my gifts, my talents, and my resources. Help me to use them well and wisely. I am ready now to energize the talent needed to achieve Creator's wish. I am open to inspiring dreams and vision. I wander in your hope-filled land.

Lesson: It is time to await opportunity expectantly or to wander seeking pieces of the dream. You are probably engaged in fantasy and longing during this period. You may even feel a craving for something you cannot quite define. There may be periods of melancholy due to the sense of uncertainty in your life right now. Flow with them. Watch them pass.

167

You will reach fulfillment on the path Creator has laid before you. Trust enough to take the first step. Let yourself be guided by dreams and visions. Look for signs. Trust your inner response. Follow that which calls you at the deepest level; respond to that which creates all-engrossing enthusiasm. Let the universe lead.

FOUR OF PIPES: Discipline, Attraction, and Preparation

Four of Pipes

Prayer: Now I use my hands to form the structure in which we shall work together. We build the lodge in which to sing and praise your powers. Great Spirit, we offer the sweat of our physical bodies, for we know it is cleansing. And we know that as we rid ourselves of poisonous fears and toxic doubts that we will be ready to celebrate with you. For the many ways of purification, we give thanks. Our love will heal and will build our desire to merge with you.

Lesson: A meeting has occurred. You are feeling the power of attraction. Your dreams and visions have brought you into contact with ones of like persuasion. Yet the forming of friendship takes discipline. The deepening of bonds requires attention. Time will now be spent developing cohesiveness. You may work together or play together. But whether in celebration or preparation, you must discipline the mind by weeding out self-doubt.

The native sweat lodge is a way of purifying your mind and body. The intense heat focuses your awareness on what is truly important and pulls out the interfering sickness of negative attitudes and fears. Ritual times of purification, letting go of all that stands between you and another, clear the way to ever-deepening love relationships.

Remember that every attraction you feel is for creative purposes. Attraction does not always imply a future of love and pairing. You are drawn together by complementary creative energies. This may or may not involve any sexual union, though it often appears, at first, as the desire for such.

You are drawn into mutual process. It is a time of enjoyment and indulgence in the pleasure of companionship. What will your indulgence bring about? What will you create together? It is an exploration time of what you can do in combination with another. Each time you experience your compatibility, you prepare yourselves to walk gracefully through later challenges.

FIVE OF PIPES:
Allure through Opposition

Prayer: It is time now to go out into the world and share my dream, to give myself to my people. I know this is a challenging time when my life could be altered by the will of others. My ideas will be up for scrutiny by those I want to please. So, Great Spirit, I accept the courage to face the world with that which you have given me. I accept the wisdom to know how to expose your divine nature within me to those who have eyes to see. I am strong in my commitment that the essence of my vision will remain true to that which you have inspired me to do. I will lure the world to its divinity by the nature of love you have given me. I will call the wild unknown, the strength and beauty ever-present within me. Your breath, your life will pass through me, and I will be at my best.

Lesson: Your vision has brought a portion of your dream to you. But not all forces are yet aligned with your dream. Your own mind may wander from your vision. You may have friends or relatives who disapprove. The world may not currently accept what you have to offer. It is time to face these things and lure the universe to accommodate you.

Holding the highest good that you can imagine in mind, begin to enter the unknown. Whether you are engaged in a hunt in the primeval forest or entering into a new marriage or a new career, you are stepping alone into a force field much larger than yourself. You are seeking only one prize, the cherished central key to your dream. Perhaps it is a person's ongoing love, maybe a position where your creative works will be recognized and encouraged, or an inner step of development that you have been longing to achieve. In any case, you must use your personal talents to guide the dearly desired toward you.

Your fears will rise up. Your expectations that others should already be attuned to your needs will be confronted. You are alone and small in a field of seeming opposition. It is time to go with your gifts, pull out your talents and use them, however meager you may think them to be. This is what the universe is asking of you now. Trust the Higher Self.

Pull out the pipes and blow your life's breath into them. Give it your all. This is the ego's battle to transcend its boundaries. It is a time of interpersonal breakthrough and growth. You are coming to terms with life around you. This is creative conflict or the therapy stage of relationship, a cleansing intensive. All of your energy is called forth to empower you. Play for all you are worth. Your Higher Self is being pulled through and the world will respond.

Remember, attachment to ego is not just self-centeredness, but can be a stubborn holding on to the old and less creative self. Free those ego boundaries. Soar beyond old limitations. There are wonderful things you wish to do. Take this chance.

SIX OF PIPES: Acceptance

Six of Pipes

Prayer: Ah, Great Spirit, I am pleased. Those aspects of my ideas that were most worthy have been accepted by my people. Those portions of my vision that I was courageous enough to accept myself have been approved by those around me. The love that I was brave enough to offer has been received. Now I take time to relax and enjoy my friendship with you. Let us play together in my love.

Lesson: It is a time of victory and peace. Those aspects of yourself that you were courageous enough to bring through by accepting them yourself have been accepted by the world. You have captured the dream. You are in a stage of equilibrium. Relax and enjoy.

Your relationship, career, or artistic expression has been accepted by the important others in your life. You have withstood the challenge and gained in strength. Conflicts are resolved. You are deemed worthy. You now have the raw materials, basic setup, or opportunity you have wanted to enable yourself to continue into higher levels of expertise. Your confidence and abilities have increased. The deer (that which you have held dear) is yours. Take it all in.

SEVEN OF PIPES:
Doubt Overcome by Action,
Spirit Freed

Seven of Pipes

Prayer: I am able now to confront my fear of loss. In every creature, I find a friend hiding behind a mask of a beast, a mask I have created by my fear. I am beginning to know this truth in everything of which I am frightened. I celebrate my success in coming to this realization. Now I face the fear of loss of what I have discovered. Yet, I know wisdom cannot be held by fear, and I must let go once again. I release my spirit and the spirits of all I encounter. I let go both of having and of losing and go forth dancing free.

Lesson: Let go. Success is but a moment's thrill. Do not be content to rest on the past, but celebrate all that was and is to come. It is easy to become complacent and to cease to expand. The more you can appreciate your achievements and quickly free your spirit once again to go on, the less the world will have to challenge your position.

There is competition for places of power that are held stubbornly. You are going to be asked to move, to grow, to continue your journey of self-awareness. So don't become attached to one stopping point. Love it while you are there, but do not hesitate to act again. Debilitating doubts creep in at every level, stagnating the flow. Dance on them. Lift yourself to new heights. You have the energy and the experience to do so.

172

A temptation when your position is challenged is to become angry or vindictive. This is a misuse of the valuable energy that is coming to you now. Eliminate envy by always leaving something for the next person to step into, a gift of your having been there first. Your protection is your ever-expanding vision that comes to include the good of all. This is a shield against jealousy and greed, against the destructive nature of anything that would seek to overcome you. You have nothing to lose if you continue to develop your skills and attune to your guiding vision, your view of the best possible world and how you play a part in it. Your acts of devotion to your own form of sexual/creative/spiritual expression is all the rebel you will ever need to be. Set your spirit free.

EIGHT OF PIPES: Your Art Is Your Shield and Power

Eight of Pipes

Prayer: Great Spirit, I am filled with light. I am burning with the fire of inspiration. I gladly take my place as your apprentice. Grant me a good teacher who will show me the way to heal with my power. I am strong enough now to overcome anger by corrective action. I am strong enough now to overcome confusion by illuminating my mind with your words. I am strong enough now to be kind even to those who do not like me. I am strong enough now to forgive those whom I thought were standing in my way. I have energy and I am powerful. My body rejoices in the pleasures you have sent me. Your gifts now fill me, for I have given myself to you,

173

Creator. You show me the way to make my life my art.

Lesson: Your creative energy is now expressing with confidence. Your past experiences now give you an edge of expertise in the area where you have focused your energy. This may be in relation to your body, its health and tone; your sexuality in relationship to others; your artistic endeavors; or in achievements of spiritual discipline such as daily yoga, tai chi, or meditation. The area in which you have chosen to channel your energy is now showing signs of your increased skill.

Enjoy the benefits of your labors and continue to direct the purpose of your process toward positive global ends. In other words, if you are using material resources, be sure you give something back to Earth. If you depend on other people's energy, be sure to replenish it in some way. If your product makes a statement, continue to upgrade the thoughts behind the statement so that it doesn't merely point out problems but also shows a way to resolution. The purpose of all energy given to you by Great Spirit is to heal. Mend the sacred hoop of life. Heal by your words, your body, your life. This is how to become a channel of the divine.

NINE OF PIPES: Relating to Power

Nine of Pipes

Prayer: I humbly take the role that I see myself in now. I gladly take the step before me. I accept this new power and position. Though people may come to me, recognizing my talents, I shall overcome the temptation to live on their compliments and stop growing. I choose instead to continue to carry out the work you place before me, Great Spirit, always accepting my highest role in relation to my people. For the place you have given me among them, I am thankful.

Lesson: You stand before your inner teacher, the power within you. You have achieved success in taking charge of your physical being, whether by controlling your diet, disciplined exercise, or fine-tuning your voice to sing, your hands to draw, your feet to dance, your fingers to play an instrument, or your heart to open to healing. You have some degree of mastery over the physical realm because you have consistently focused your energy in a certain direction. You may be a mother of children or a mother of invention. Whatever you have done, you are on the threshold of a deeper relationship with the Great Power.

You are at a point where you will feel the gift of increased energy, a bonus for work well done thus far. However, the intensity of this gift may cause anxiety or confusion if you do not understand its purpose. It is as if you have been playing the game and suddenly the ball is in your hands. Excitement pours through you. Don't panic. Just go for your larger goal. It is time to act.

Pitfalls here involve wanting to eliminate the unusual energy or wasting it on excesses such as overeating, drinking too much, drug indulgence, or compulsive, non-meaningful sexual activity in lieu of taking the action your soul really wants you to take. The extra energy must be used courageously to move you forward into the wholeness, into a place in your highest fantasy. You can live your dream if you take your next step bravely now.

Bring your high ideals home to bless your foundation. Your power is great and must be put to good purpose.

TEN OF PIPES: Coming Home

Ten of Pipes

Prayer: The people honor me today. They honor the work that you have given me to do and I have done. I have completed one task. Now, once again, I am free to choose. I can go on to a new level with my work; or I can change here and explore my life with you in another way. But now, I enjoy this moment of glory. Great Spirit, for you I dance tonight, for you I paint, I write. For you my life continues, and for the children who seek my blessing.

Lesson: Your life has been a series of adventures. You have earned health and a wealth of experience. Now you come home to rest and to integrate the many experiences you have collected. You are full of ideas, so many you may not know where to begin to implement them all. You want to give back to the world, to teach others, to pass on your knowledge accumulated so far.

You have acquired the artist's eye, the poet's heart, or

176

the musician's ear. You are both fulfilled and at a point of new beginning. Take time for yourself. This is a turning point. You have just reached a plateau and will soon step to a new level.

APPRENTICE OF PIPES: Channeling the Light

Apprentice of Pipes

Prayer: I open now to the message that comes from within. I shall be brave in carrying out the Spirit's call. This time I light my pipe having come a long way, another leg of my journey complete. I take time here to pause and renew my vision. I seclude myself so that my inner words shall be clear. Then, I will take up my pack and walk again, knowing my way. My body now is a channel, an instrument of light, and wherever I go, whatever my talent, I shall inspire others by my manner of being. I open to the flow as I feel it within me.

Lesson: At this point, though you may be well-known for what you have done, you begin a new level of study. You work with a true master, on either the inner or the outer planes. Your body will learn to further refine its talents.

What is the message you came to deliver to the world? Every fiber of your being is now going to learn to express it. You no longer depend so much on the instruments of your trade; you have mastered them. Now, you depend on the instrument of Self. Your body becomes a clear channel, energy freely flowing. You are a student again, but filled with grace.

TOTEM OF PIPES:
Eagle, the Flyers

Totem of Pipes

EAGLE
THE FLYERS

Prayer: I am a warrior of the inner realms, striking out against the errors I see with my beam of tranquility. I am an artist at life. Yet, still, life teaches me every day to sharpen my skills. I am learning to create in the outer world the inner world I see. I am a student, eager to succeed, for success brings light to the darkness. Yet, I know that even while I contain the truth and am anxious to make change, I must be patient and walk in balance. I must keep the inner peace. I am learning to have the eagle's eye, to watch quietly until it is time to act impeccably.

Lesson: There are things to learn from all kingdoms of nature. The eagle flies higher than any bird, thus has become a symbol of higher vision, seeing the total picture. All of the flyers have wings. They rise above humans, using their energy to soar on the winds. You will be coming into contact with one of the flyers. Learn from them. Watch and listen. Let them be your teacher now. Practice what they teach.

POWER LODGE OF THE PIPES:
Wise Priestess Energizing Others

Prayer: This is my peak of excellence in living a spiritual truth. I am able to give of my wisdom to others who come my way. I empower others by encouraging their own talents and abilities, giving opportunity to the potential within them. As I observe the qualities of God within, I bring them forth. In my creative work, I have found you, Creator, living and giving life to all I do. My art is my heart, filled with love for you. And all who receive my art are thereby blessed. This work I give. In beauty I live. I have expressed one quality of you. You are the power that has attracted all I love. I am the power of you.

Lesson: You are adept in the use of your creative/sexual/spiritual energy. You have gained access to power. Your challenge is to handle it humbly, considering the good of all. You cannot deny your beauty, expertise, creative achievement, or quality of craftsmanship, but you are still a human being learning to fully carry out Creator's plan. The purpose of the wand that has been handed to you is to cast a magic spell of hope on the world. The purpose of carrying the pipe is to assist others in using their sexual/creative/spiritual energy in a masterful way.

Use your power to praise Mother Nature's creation, to acknowledge the Source, to herald the dawn of a peaceful age, to uplift those who cannot yet see. Use your power to heal, to love unconditionally. Devote yourself to serving the Spirit within all that lives.

This is the prime of your energy. You have taken the wild energy of youth into mature forms of expression. The more you have truly expressed the energy of Self within you, the more youthful vitality you take into physical maturity. You must not deny Self, but merely find the right channel for ongoing, expanding expression. This is the lesson you have learned and must encourage others to learn. Each has an individual way. Be aware and bring it forth.

EXEMPLAR OF THE PIPES: The Sage Is a Self Well-Expressed

Prayer: The time ends for my active work in this area. Yet I shall live a long time to tell of all I know. Those who come to me for advice, I will inspire with my vision's fulfillment. I have lived a brave life and passed the tests of time. I have brought forth all of the beauty within me on the path of my purpose. My art now guides the world toward right relationship to all that is. I am free now to take up a new path. But while I am here, I will lead with love and kindness. I will pass on what I know. Ancient ancestors, guide me on to the golden road so that I do not get lost in past glory. Keep me aware of new days to come. Make me a child again.

Lesson: You have earned the title Sage or Creative Genius. You are a visionary who has lived life fully and well, the artist at life itself. Your works will last long beyond your own physical life and thus are immortal. You are passing on the pipe now, handing down the wand. This may be in only one area of your life or all of them. You know.

180

It is an end time. But it is also a time when you reign supreme. Be wise. You will be asked to pass on. It is a good time to reflect, to be thankful, to make completions. Do not get caught up in the feeling of "dying." There is no death that lasts. Your life conditions, the context in which you find your Self, simply change. Let go of your identification with the earlier parts of your journey. You are not the journey. You are not the past. You are not a has-been or a once-was. You are vital in the here and now. You are an Exemplar of the Pipes. You are a living example of that on which you spent your life energy. You will be given a new life where the long-term benefits of your work support you. Future generations will live with creations developed through your energy. You will be a child among them. The fulfillment of Self well-expressed becomes the art that inspires and guides the world. You will be born again in the future of your own creation.

Arrows

In older tarot decks, this suit is commonly referred to as swords. Within the word "swords" is the word "words." This is an easy way to remember just what it is that causes or relieves struggle. In some tarot books, you will find the suit of swords referring oftentimes to struggle or conflict. Now we are learning that our words, thoughts, and attitudes create our reality of conflict or peace. Before you learn to take command of your words and the combinations of words that are your beliefs and attitudes, the sword is an appropriate symbol for them. Your words, like swords, get you into and out of trouble.

But as you learn to take charge of your mind power, your words become arrows directed at a specific target and released with a particular energy. The point of your words must be to direct thought-energy to its most inspiring and uplifting level. The words of a great poet or storyteller are good examples. They encourage right action from all who hear them.

The lessons of the Arrows suit will bring you toward mastery of your mind, helping you to get what you need in life and to give what life needs from you. Your struggles will tell you when your thoughts are off the mark. Each Arrow card will help you re-aim, to realign your mind with One Mind, the cosmic bull's eye.

When your mind is aimed at the highest target, you will be magnetically drawn toward that which will cause you to take action in behalf of reaching that target. The mind is not simply a magic tool that, once thinking positively, will cause life to bring treats to your doorstep without you taking action. It is, instead, a powerful magnet that will draw opportunity to you in the area of your aims and goals. You must pursue them with continued proper attitude. Again, the words that you continue to dwell on while carrying out actions designate the kind of experience you will have during that action.

In other words, it is not enough to plan and make affirmations of what you want. You must take opportunities when they come and be mindful of right attitude—appreciation and full participation—while you act. When you are finished with the experience, you must hold words of self-acceptance about what you have done and begin again to plan and affirm the next step.

The suit of Arrows calls you to undertake a great mental discipline. But the rewards of a life of integrity and clear direction are well worth the effort. As time goes by in your journey through the Arrows, you will see that the point of it all—the result of your right mindfulness, right action—is to become a sage who passes wisdom on to future generations through words and example. Your words must guide and teach all who do not yet know those things you have spent your life discovering.

ACE OF ARROWS:
Will to Do

Ace of Arrows

Prayer: The arrow of my mind I aim toward God. Bow in hand, I am ready for anything I encounter. So filled am I with daring, I welcome challenge. I have words to guide me. I have a voice that can be heard. I can see the distant target and feel certain of my aim. I have thought, and thought is my power. I have will, and I will do. From my mind I weed all doubt, for the experience of life will be my teacher and, falling, I will pick myself up; noticing error, I will make correct. I can do what I will, for I trust the will of the Highest, which is known within me.

Lesson: This is the card of original thought, the basic "I am." It is the beginning of the power to will. Here you discover your blueprint for this life's work. "I will myself to be" brought you into this existence. Now you will get in touch with the form this life's reality will take through your being.

Your consciousness is penetrated by thought. You have the gift of intelligence, the power to shape words into a combination that will release energy in you to go forth. You have been given many words (concepts) by your culture of birth. Some of them may no longer be useful for you. They may be interfering with your good now, whereas previously they may have helped you to survive your

183

particular situation. You are at a point of taking charge. You will begin to probe deeply into the workings of your own mind.

Throughout the suit of Arrows, you will find the coyote, often known as "the trickster." Thoughts are also tricksters. They can fool you. Modern day advertising is a clear example of how words can be arranged to make you feel you are getting something you are not. People in your life may also use words to fool you, or even themselves, into believing that you are at fault, you should do something that you feel you shouldn't, and such things as this. Become aware of the power of words to do these things. Notice when your own words are out of alignment with how you are really feeling. Truth is a combination of several ingredients. It is congruence between your feelings and what you say. It is also saying what you feel in the way that most recognizes the principle of divinity in all things. In other words, tact and right timing are part of speaking the truth. Knowing your whole self is its basis.

The owl in the suit of Arrows stands for wisdom. Wisdom looks at experience and the effect of words on all who hear them. Wisdom decides a course of action based on the experience of Self and the Wisdom of Ages. Trickster words may cause you to take whatever action gets you an immediate benefit without regard for the outcome or its effect on others. Words of wisdom will have the ring of the teachings of the masters of life. They will sound eternal, applicable through many situations, many ages, many times.

Words can heal or steal. Now is the time to contemplate just what the words you hold in your mind are doing for you and to others. What meaning are you giving your life as you define your experience to yourself? How are you valuing what you do? You are not the words themselves.

You are in control of them. They are your tools. You will become the master craftswoman with them. Words describe life, but you are the willpower behind them. Only you can act on them. Aim to take command.

TWO OF ARROWS: Aim High

Two of Arrows

Prayer: I have studied the map of mind. I am off to take charge of my world. In the midst of my enthusiasm, I take time out to make sure the highest goal can still be seen. My motivations are clear. I am seeking the best for all. I accept help from those who have blazed the trail before me. I set my heart on a course of love. I desire plenty for all. My sights are set high above the common thought. Great Spirit, your will dwells within as my highest aspirations. Lead me now on the course of making them real.

Lesson: Aim toward your highest vision. Be poised for success. You are in charge. No one else can think your thoughts for you. People can offer suggestions, ideas, and teachings, but you are the bottom line. You are the final authority, author of your own intellectual life. You accept or reject everything you hear, see, and experience. You give it its value. You claim it and thus give it its power to affect your life. Pull your good toward you by aiming at what you really want.

As you aim high, your Higher Self or Soul is called to assist you. She is the magical Grandmother who brings plenty to your life. She is that part of you that possesses the wisdom of the ages. This higher portion of yourself is trying her best to activate you toward providing well for yourself and others. Listen to her now.

THREE OF ARROWS: Listen to Your Heart

Three of Arrows

Prayer: I allow the information I need to come to my senses by paying attention to what is before me. I see that the world gives me whatever is needed if I simply open my eyes and ears. The world is giving me constant feedback on the thoughts I hold in my mind. It provides clues to where I might find what I am looking for. I pause. I listen. I follow my heart. Grandmother, guide me with the star-bright song of your timeless way. I seek to bring plenty to my people.

Lesson: Your thoughts must travel through your heart. If your action began with attunement to the "I Am" mind of the all-perfect universe, then what is coming to you now should be plenty of what you want. The buffalo is the North American Native symbol of plenty. It provided food, clothing, and shelter materials for many tribes. It was respected, fully utilized, and appreciated. When it was around, no one went without. Consider the needs of your people in your aims.

If you find yourself with plenty of disappointment, it is time to look to your thoughts again and into your heart. Did you set out to achieve a goal your heart was not into? Did you override deep feelings within? Were your goals overlooking the needs of others? Are there unkind words now piercing your heart and limiting your vision? Listen.

Words can be stab words (s-words) or salve words—"I

don't like you," or "I forgive you." Your sword (words) can cut away the problem or wound the one with whom you are experiencing the problem. Pay attention. Aim to foster love.

FOUR OF ARROWS: Contemplate Your Blessings

Four of Arrows

Prayer: Grandmother, I realize that the road that has been traveled most may not be the one on which I shall find my game. The structure that is already standing may need to be changed to suit my purposes. In my mind, I create anew. I am a seed of a new culture, a world yet to come. Wisdom, come whisper while I sit tying up the threads of my life. I seek to make best use of all resources, to express my true nature, and to teach what I learn to those who follow this road behind me.

Lesson: Take time to organize your thoughts. Allow your recent experiences to integrate with your prior knowledge and future visions by becoming still. Meditate, contemplate, write in your journal, perhaps sleep and dream. Pull back from trying to achieve so that you can get an overall view of things. You may be very logical and rational at first, but then free yourself of figuring things out and just float into fantasy. Get out of the stream of purposeful activity. If you do something, do it only for the enjoyment of itself in the moment. This is a mental discipline. Let wisdom come while you rest.

Look at what you have to work with. Play with what is at hand. Have no thought of results for now. Live today within your means, and see if it can be peaceful there. Everything you have, your thoughts have brought you. The road that has been traveled by others may not lead you to your own destination. Appreciate the uniqueness of your being and allow your own path to unfold before you. Appreciate the rewards that your own way of life bring to you.

FIVE OF ARROWS: Noticing Needs

Five of Arrows

Prayer: Great Spirit, I see that now that I have provided so well for myself, others envy what I have gained. My possessions are sought by others in need. Grant me the wisdom to help them satisfy their real longings and to provide for themselves the things they desire. Grant me the faith to continue my own way and to leave no one wanting behind me. I shall revise my plan to include new knowledge you give me. I accept further understanding you will give me so that harmony, once again, will reign.

Lesson: Though you may have created a nice life for yourself, the universe will not let you stop there. Your basic beliefs will be challenged until your personal philosophy takes into account the needs of others . . . more and more others the farther along you go. On the other hand, if you have not learned to take care of yourself, your intellect will be challenged to find a suitable set of concepts that will work for you.

You are going to be asked to face the world head on. You have set out on a course of action, and it is time to view the results. This can be a frightening time, when you are tempted to throw out your own way of doing things, if results are not as you had hoped, and to adopt another belief system without critical consideration. Rather than becoming a quick convert, it is better to look at your own way with a critical eye, and fine-tune the places where it could use improvement.

You have built a foundation. Your way has brought you this far. Even if you are laughed at the first time you present yourself publicly, you must realize that the presentation was the only way to actualize any new form. When the audience laughs, the worst is over. You have now gained the insight necessary to revise your plan, refine your act, and step forth once again in confidence.

Your success could bring jealousy, envy, or criticism from others, yet your generous urge to share what you have may be the wrong move here. Be sure you pass on what others truly need to better their own condition.

SIX OF ARROWS:
End Struggle

Six of Arrows

Prayer: I take time now to reflect on that which I have done. I have met a challenge. The struggle is ended. But my consciousness seeks to overcome the conditions that lead to this struggle in all beings. My mind must float a while in new waters. Though I can care for myself, I must find a way in which that self-caring can also encompass others. I enter new territory as I decide to readjust my aim, to shift my course so that it encompasses even greater wisdom than I have gleaned thus far. Come now, light of fresh insight; take me to the mountain.

Lesson: Let go of the past, the immediate past as well as those ghosts of childhood. You may have had a humbling experience just when you thought you were on top of the world. Leave the sorrow behind and go forth in peace knowing a greater understanding is ahead. You are entering an expansive period.

With the help of others, you are going to know life from a greater perspective. Look ahead. Leave broken dreams behind. The pieces will reform into portions of a new dream at a later time. Trust the flow of life as it takes you forward.

It is a good time to meditate. Seek higher wisdom. Stop the flow of old thoughts. Look to the light. You had to reach this plateau before you could climb higher. Your first goal reached, your sights must be set higher. Cast away fear and doubt as you flow forward toward the dawn.

SEVEN OF ARROWS:
Listen to the Truths of
the Sages

Seven of Arrows

Prayer: Grandmothers, Grandfathers, open your ways to me. I will practice and perfect them in my peaceful place within. I understand that I am the translator of all your words for the world in which I am living. Speak to my heart, my soul. Let seeker and wisdom be one. All thanks be to you who have walked before me.

Lesson: You are finding through your experience that some of the truths you were taught in the past are of real value.

Though you may have left the religion of your childhood and set aside some of your early training, you are finding support from the sages. Ancient ways are being revealed to you through your own life events.

You have questioned. You have let go of that which did not benefit you. You are now edging beyond skepticism of all systems of thought and coming to see one light uniting them all. You are opening to the Masters of Wisdom as they reveal their truths in response to your everyday concerns. Can you be humble enough to accept the words of those who have lived their lives to reveal divine wisdom to you?

Reclaim that which empowers you. You now understand how certain beliefs help or hinder you. Take into yourself those ways of thinking that enhance your life and its greatest purpose. Do not be afraid to adopt the ways of the wise.

EIGHT OF ARROWS: Commitment to a Way

Eight of Arrows

Prayer: My tools are now within. I am master of my mind, and I give my knowledge that others may master their lives. I live by the creed of words within me. No battle inside or conflict outside will frighten me. I can do what I believe I must. I give what it takes to restore and renew. I have been called and I answer. From perfect peace, I take my call. My will and the will of the Father are one. In Mother, the world of matter, my gifts are offered.

Lesson: You have advanced to a new perspective. From here you will empower others by offering a means to their greater well-being. You will give gifts that continue to give of their own nature. Now that you have a new philosophy, religion, or lifestyle (each of these describes a large body of words you live by), you must realize that it will restrict you in certain ways. Initially, you will be blind to those restrictions, but in time you will notice. At that point, you must realize the power of restriction. Commitment can be freedom.

You must realize that there is no way to be completely unrestricted and still be living. Each belief system fences you in and at the same time frees you to do things you could not do otherwise. For instance, the concept of marriage may restrict you to experiencing sexuality with just one partner. But it frees you to go with that partner to peaks of intimacy which would not be available to you otherwise. The concept of being a vegetarian may restrict you from eating meat, but free you to experience the increased physical energy and heightened consciousness you can know only through a body purified by live, whole foods. The concept of dressing for success may limit your creative expression, but can land you a high-paying job. So you can see the value of knowing the power of restriction.

You are not searching now, in this area of your life, but have a workable philosophy in which your commitment will free your spirit to reach previously unreachable goals.

NINE OF ARROWS:
Overcome Doubt and Fear

Nine of Arrows

Prayer: I can see through sorrows; I can see through struggles. What I find is mind. The mental concepts, the attitudes, the beliefs I hold, I cherish for what they have allowed me to do. But I also see that they are simply ways of perceiving reality and not reality itself. The only reality is ultimate harmony, and troubles are simply trips the mind is taking. As I stumble on the path, I put myself down and I pick myself up by the way I value each step. I am way above rules, though not above using them. I am deeply respectful of all that is; I laugh at all that isn't. Even blind, I can see that worries are clouds drifting past eternity.

Lesson: The world appears to oppress its people. Darkness abounds. Yet you can penetrate those clouds of worry and fear by aiming into the light. You do not need to see all answers and have all solutions before you act. Just point your heart toward good.

Perhaps you have found something you did not expect. You have looked into the darkness and found your own greatest fear. You are being shown what you have placed in the shadows of your consciousness. What you wanted to forget has raised its head, but only to ask if you have gained enough wisdom and strength to deal with it more fully.

It may seem like a nightmare at first. You may not want to look at it. But you must accept your dark side, your hidden desires and integrate them with your light side in order to experience wholeness. You are never given a

193

challenge that you do not have the skills to meet. It may seem as though you are shooting in the dark, but go ahead. Use the skills you have been working to develop. This is their supreme test.

A new surge of power awaits your success. The mask is lifted as you look behind the face of things to see that your fear was merely self-doubt rather than an external enemy. Take heart. Lift your bow of confidence, and shoot pure thoughts of love, strength, and highest vision. Aim for the good of the whole.

TEN OF ARROWS: Steadfast Mind

Ten of Arrows

Prayer: Having developed my body, taken charge of my thoughts, and risen above the struggle of life, I am in command. I fully accept my leadership role. My training is complete. Now, I can wear the cloak of success where all can freely view me. It is in this role that others may criticize, envy, and attempt to overthrow my power. But I lead in confidence, knowing that if I keep my eye on the goal and my heart in your hands, Great Spirit, I cannot fail. I am centered in peace and my will is my power. My shield is my positive thought. My still mind keeps me from all disruption. Thanks be to those lessons I have been given.

Lesson: False friends cannot harm you. Though your ego may feel attacked, your philosophy will see you through. Your leadership is being resisted. Every positive idea you have had is being met with equal and negative force, but hold steady. You have come a long way to develop your

194

belief system. You have probably reached a point where you thought you "had it all together." This current resistance by others may be an unexpected turn of events, but your True Self will shine through. Everything unnecessary will fall away, including false friends.

Hold to your truth. Stand fast in love. You may feel humbled and your ego-self may not like what is happening, but do not give way to anger, resentment, and thoughts of a lower nature. Your target is God-realization, not revenge.

The warrior's path is straight and clear. She simply does not waver from the good.

Apprentice of Arrows

APPRENTICE OF ARROWS: Brave Herald of New Thought

Prayer: I speak in words that affirm the positive. I write in words that speak the truth, knowing that truth is the underlying goodness within creation, and anything less than wondrous is false. I dismiss all thoughts of "I can't" and feelings that I am not responsible. I throw off whatever limits my good and the good of those around me. I see beauty and I speak to beauty. I see love and I speak to love. Where I cannot see these, I supply them. Bravely I go forth and change the words that cause harm, grief or hunger. I change the laws. I change limits. I re-view concepts; I re-mind myself. I re-create a better place to play. I am a messenger bringing new thoughts that are the seeds of freedom. With the words you give me, Great Spirit, the young shall be liberated, the world transformed.

Lesson: Your words live forever in the hearts and minds of seven generations. Speak in such a way that their minds can develop images of better ways. In guiding anyone, particularly youth, make sure your words assist their becoming self-responsible, capable and caring.

Listen to the needs of the developing soul of the student, just as you have been listened to by the ever-present Guiding Beings who stand by you in total love. Encourage the expression of Highest Self in all beings. Point the way by your own life and actions. You will return to life in the world you have given your children.

Teach that all can be transformed. The young have come to correct the errors of your generation. Give them the skills to do so. They are hope. Give them faith in themselves. Inspire courage. Share the wisdom that has helped you on your own path and the wisdom that you have developed. Point the way. Encourage harmonious action. There is a child somewhere awaiting the knowledge you hold.

TOTEM OF ARROWS: Coyote, the Four Leggeds

Totem of Arrows

COYOTE
THE FOUR LEGGEDS

Prayer: Through all my battles, I have come. On a hard path, I have traveled. With mountain below, I sit at the peak. The clouds are my pillows now. The sun is my crown. And I will sit here until my teachings are heard, never ceasing to speak. Those with ears to hear will feel my wild and cunning nature. I am free, yet determined. I know my way and seize every opportunity that comes on my path. The spirit moves me.

Lesson: The coyote has been known as "The Trickster." There is no greater trickster than words. If you can learn their power, you have mastered a tremendous force. People often trick themselves into believing they have achieved a goal simply because they can verbalize it. But words must be backed by full commitment of action to achieve.

People are also tricked into believing that they are the words others use to describe them. You are not what others think of you. You are the words you allow to dwell in your mind. People are persuaded by words, believing in false promises. You must not only listen, but observe. Do others act in accord with the words you hear them speaking? Do you? Trust not words alone, but the power behind them. Listen to the essence of what is being spoken.

Your body often knows truth before your mind does. Like the four-leggeds, you have an inner sense of when to pay attention. Your instinctive body response senses danger, pleasure, promise. It knows when to exercise caution, restraint, abandon, frivolity, grace, cunning. Learn its way. Listen with your whole body.

TEACHING LODGE OF THE ARROWS:
Liberator

Prayer: In the name of harmony and peace I live. I am the one who speaks. I have studied the great warriors, the peacemakers, those who freed slaves, and those who stood their own ground. I am learning the themes of their lives and making them my own. I am learning from revolutionary women and evolutionary men the very qualities that gave them undying spirit. I am gathering to myself the knowledge that I, too, can draw on the Great Mind. In my life, I will correct an injustice, I will right a wrong. I will bring love where none has been known. I attune myself to the sound of truth; and I listen until I am known.

Lesson: It is time to put yourself in the company of great minds. Whether through books, films, or person-to-person, surround yourself with heroic presence. Read the words of those who mastered life. Listen to music that fills you with positive visions. Let poetry enter and inspire you.

Delete from your reality the sounds and images that bring you down. At least in your personal space, surround yourself with visual, auditory, and sensory experiences that uplift. Create your own Teaching Lodge of the Arrows. No bad news here, no television, no newspapers, no magazines that do not support your highest aspirations. It is time to create, at least in your own small space, a completely inspiring environment. Then welcome God and Goddess.

EXEMPLAR OF THE ARROWS: Master Storyteller

Prayer: Once upon a time, I lived a warrior's life. I strived. I sought. I conquered my fears. I saved the lives of others who were fearful by helping them to be brave. And all the way, I enjoyed myself. So I am here to talk about it. Hear my stories and you will learn my warrior's way. Listen to my life and you will find the way that is your own to travel. For I am kind and can see all ways. I have risen high up to the sky and soar with eagles to watch you. I have dug into the soil of my soul and grown. I have traveled by instinct to journey's end, and floated in peace in the night. My eyes are above the world, but my stories are in it. Thus, I can teach, and my words will be beautiful.

Lesson: The Exemplar has lived and thus passes on wisdom, not empty words. Back up your beliefs with experience. This is the only way to test for truth.

The Exemplar is the Master Storyteller, a sage and wise one whose words empower. It is time to encourage the young, clarify possibilities for a balanced future, and disseminate pure thought. You have cast out doubt and despair. Now you can reveal hopes that can be made real by those who follow you. Speak of the world worth working for.

Your words pave the way to the future. Your experience tells you which words hold fast through time. Your thoughts are pure, for they are based on a reality you understand fully by the life you have lived. They are not in conflict with what is, but encompass and describe it.

199

Bowls

This suit, also known as cups, is best symbolized by some kind of container. It could be a cup, bowl, basket, chalice, or any vessel that serves to remind you to empty yourself each day that you might have room to be refilled. This minor mystery of life, the mystery of emptiness and fulfillment, loneliness and all-one-ness, surrounds you each day. The lessons teach you to realize that your own body/mind is the container of love. Within you are worlds and beings, lands and adventures that guide your everyday life.

The Bowls ask you to come on a journey of devotion, to recognize that you have been given time, and time is the road on which you lay your life day by day. Through time, you are to love. Lessons come your way and you are to live each one in the highest love that you can generate, offering every life experience to that embodiment of all love, the Great Spirit within. Spirit dwells everywhere and it is up to you to find it. You have been given a life of Time in which to do so.

How you spend your time is how you love. What you spend your time doing is that to which you are devoted. What you are devoted to is your religion. Your religion is your spiritual expression. It does not have to be formal and dogmatic. Life is to be your love, your expression, your devotion. Every moment is an opportunity for sacrament or sacrifice. You can make life sacred or profane.

The Bowls ask you to look at what you carry with you. What fills you? What nourishes you? To whom do you offer sustenance? To whom do you offer your cup of love, your basket of life's harvest? The bowl that carries the food of your life to your body is either simple or luxurious. Either way, it is a sign of the life you are living. What does it say about you? Do you take more than you need? More than you offer? Does anyone go hungry because you eat? These are the questions asked by the suit of Bowls. You will now discover how you answer them.

ACE OF BOWLS:
Offering of Love

Ace of Bowls

Prayer: In our hearts, we are peace. Within us dwells this spirit which brings joy to all who would seek the highest good. It is the best for ourselves and others. The divine perfection is already within our beings. The hand of inner helpers is always ready to reach out and lift us up. We must, however, ask for this help. We must pause to find that peaceful place within . . . there does the divine idea dwell. If we reach out, offering love to others, our spiritual gifts are pulled up from within us and reach our consciousness. As we give, the inner waters flow and guide us to harmony. The nectar of Infinite Love is already in our hearts. From this I drink deeply now.

Lesson: Inside you there is a Giver of Love. You may think of this giver as higher than you, other than you, more godly, pure, an essence of spirit, but you can only find hir through yourself. You must go inside, dwell in your inner space, in order to make contact. Inner and outer are simply convenient thought constructs that order our world a certain way. It does not matter which way you perceive yourself to be going. God is in every direction.

The ace of Bowls asks you to recognize your ability to be in touch with the giver of love and recognize that you are an extension of that One. What you offer anyone or any situation is a gift from that giver if you are dwelling in that place of love inside yourself.

Recognize that you have something to offer. Accept your inner gifts, your intentions of love and your desire to love. Now is the time to contemplate kindness, attention, acceptance, emotional comfort and sustenance. These are all forms of love with no strings attached. In order to give freely and without expectation you must find the source of constant replenishment inside yourself. If you cannot easily find that Giver, make one up. Your imagination is the bridge you build so that higher being can get to you. Do not be afraid to build a good one. Remember, God, Goddess and Guides are formless beings. You give them the form in which they can appear to you. It is easier for us humans, especially Western minds, to form personally fulfilling relationships with someone we can "see." So don't be afraid to allow Infinite Love to take form according to your desires. After all, that is what you are trying to do when you look for a true friend or love partner. You are asking the Giver of Love to embody before you as a person to whom you can relate. Embody the Giver of Love within you first, and the outer world will supply all you need.

TWO OF BOWLS: Friendship

Prayer: There is always one who awaits the gift of myself. No human can live without this sharing of her humanness. One kind word can make all the difference in the world, one small gift can change a life. I am open to receiving. I am ready to give. As these aspects of giving and receiving become friends within myself, my true friends appear in my earthly life. I will make the gesture now that will show another I am friend. Together, through our relationship, we shall heal and become strong.

Lesson: You must conceive of love with another. You must imagine friendship before you can have it. What do you have to offer another? Can you pay attention to another person, listening, following their words, feeling their feelings? Can you imagine what it would be like to be that person?

Just for a minute, think of someone you know. Mock their body position, facial expressions, common things you hear them say. Never do this in front of them, of course, because you will always be a poor representation of their wholeness. But while you are alone, just act like that person for a few minutes, and you will get instant insight into some of the reasons they are who they are.

A relationship is an exercise in balance. You have needs and wishes, your partner has needs and wishes. Sometimes you must lead, sometimes follow. In the best of situations, you each have strengths that can be utilized by the relationship. Where one has a strong desire to handle some aspect of living, the other may have little interest.

This is an excellent situation for encouraging one person to take charge and the other to enhance that one's strength with support and encouragement. Each person must have areas where they are the final authority in the relationship. And each person must be supported in that role in their area of expertise and feel that area to be an important and meaningful one.

Authority must not be decided by outdated role models. It is not an "I'm up; you're down" situation. Authority comes with skill, interest, enthusiasm and the ability to take responsibility. Think now of the ways you and your partner can enhance each other's strengths.

THREE OF BOWLS: Spiritual Kinship

Three of Bowls

Prayer: Whenever others are gathered around me, I will celebrate our lives. In groups, in front of others, is never the time to criticize another, but to praise them. In this way, all are lifted up. As we share that which we like and appreciate about each other, our bowls are filled with heavenly grace. Let us be thankful together for all that we have been given as human beings on Earth in this time. Let us share our bounty. Let us share our blessings. Only through sharing does abundance come.

Lesson: Can you attend to the needs of the group as a whole? This is the question asked by this card. Love is something to be shared. Kin, or spiritual family, are those people whose souls you have seen. They are not simply social contacts, business acquaintances, nor necessarily people with common interests. Instead, they are people in whom you have recognized the invisible qualities of God. They have touched you emotionally and you feel grateful.

Now is the time to let them know how much you appreciate them. What could you do for a friend today that would let hir know you have seen hir high self? The waters of consciousness unite with the family of man, woman, and all creation. What flows from you will in the great circle of life eventually flow to you as well. Send out your love to someone near. Love will return to you from afar.

FOUR OF BOWLS:
Materialization of Love

Four of Bowls

Prayer: To my mind, as I am at rest, come wonderful thoughts of things I shall like to create for others to show my love for them. In my mind when I am at peace, Creator tells me of what it is I have to share. It is through my own talents and abilities, through my own use of these in time, that I create those gifts I imagined. Now I give form to the love I feel for another. Now I create my gift in a material way, expressing those intangible feelings that draw me to my people.

Lesson: At this point in your relationship with someone, the spirit moves you to bring your love into a form. This form could take many different shapes. It could simply be a gift you make and offer as a statement of your feelings. It could be a contract formalizing your relationship with one another. It could be a first touch, a deeper level of contact, a commitment. Whatever it is, it involves you a little more.

You are manifesting, that is, making material in the outer world, some quality of experience within you. The valentine is the simplest Western symbol of love. If it is made by your hands, it has been touched with your love. Touch only to express the love you feel. And remember the source. Your cup is always filled by the Giver of Love within. If another human being expresses love to you, that is a gift, simply extra frosting on the cake. Your love is not dependent on it. Your rewards and refills are equal to the amount you allow your true being to express in all the other areas of your life. This allowing of your highest nature is what brings your love to its pure unconditionality. Love thyself, then give freely from this love.

FIVE OF BOWLS: Letting Go

Five of Bowls

Prayer: I accept now the courage to go forth, offering my self to the world. I know that through my very presentation, I will be changed; and I trust that this change will be for my greatest good. I am in tune with the source of all love, and I know that no love given is truly lost, for it is infinitely replaced by the Great Keeper and Giver of Love to all. I trust, Great Spirit, that in all giving that flows forth from my own being, you are the true receiver. I now allow the gifts with which you have filled me to travel outward to the world.

Lesson: The presentation of your heartfelt feeling may or may not be accepted. Not everyone will understand or seem open to you. The fear of rejection often keeps us from giving fully of ourselves to others. What if they should not like our gifts? What if they should laugh and make fun? Only through rejection are we compelled to reflect and improve, to seek the learning that perhaps we have been lacking. It is the refiner's fire through which we must come. Yet it is often our own lack of confidence that draws to us that rejection. Where we are certain of our motivation and competent in our expression, others accept us.

The five of Bowls is providing a situation where we are forced to reexamine our motives. Life may be asking you to change your manner of presentation. The words or gestures you used therein may have been misinterpreted by the receiver of your intentions. What words did s/he want to hear? What has s/he really asked from you? Do not give what *you* need; give what the other needs.

On the other hand, to the very best of your understanding, upon self-reflection, you may see nothing you could have done differently. The person may simply not be able to receive what you offer. They are closed to your efforts. Can you let go without blame? No use stopping up your flow of kindness, generosity, and care. Just redirect it. There are millions of people desperate for any act of love. The world is full of needy.

If you cannot find someone to love unselfishly, you are truly asleep, and it is definitely time to open your eyes. Feed the hungry. Care for the sick. Be merciful. Offer what you have. If you have a tendency to feel rejected, give your love to someone who would appreciate it most. This could be a child, an older person, or anyone your society tends to overlook or abuse.

Whatever you do, do it and let go. Your rewards should be constantly happening within you as you let your highest qualities come through. Results are nice, but do not wait up for them. Keep going. You have just primed the pump. Much greater things are to come because whether or not you know it at the conscious level, you have learned a lesson. The lesson will self-correct your system. Trust the unwavering tendency of your being to seek better and better situations for you. You will find your hidden strength.

SIX OF BOWLS:
Appreciate Days Gone By

Six of Bowls

Prayer: I have given my gift of love, and it has been gratefully received by another. In the waters of life, we rest our desires and allow ourselves to be moved by a greater force. It is in this time of looking back that we realize life is perfect and that we are prepared to meet whatever will come our way. Endless streams of emotion flow between myself and the beloved you placed within my reach. We are consciously united in the great pleasure that is but a taste of the wonder of God. Great Spirit, I give thanks for this universe full of treasures that you give to me through all in my love's care. With each person whom I love and with whom I share my inner being, I come to know yet another part of your great glory.

Lesson: You may be feeling a little nostalgia, longing for days gone by, loves experienced and lost. But nothing is truly lost. The lessons of that love live on. Be thankful. Life has given you some exquisite moments. Remember them and honor them. They have been your teachers.

It might be time to reconnect with an old lover, a childhood sweetheart, a friend far away. Relive your dreams and let learning occur. It may be time to forgive, to make amends. Sights, sounds, tastes, smells, images will remind you of long ago. Pay attention to them now. In some way, symbolically or ritually honor what has been. This encapsulates it for you and stores it in your mind and body as a good medicine power. Digest that whole period of your life or that whole relationship of your past into one powerful symbol, song, poem, or dance, or project it into a stone, a painting, a photo collage, a woven cloth, or any other cherished object. Your life will become your art by so doing, and your art will become your life.

Romance comes when the past is completed. To the extent that the past is left unfinished, unappreciated, unforgiven, your next partner will be plagued by your illusions and fears. A kind goodby to what once was cleanses the cup to be filled with fresh love once again.

SEVEN OF BOWLS:
Swept Away

Seven of Bowls

Prayer: Time has brought me ever deeper into relationship with my true love partner. More and more, Great Spirit, we realize that this is you. In each of us you live and manifest your beauty. Our blessings are great, but we know there is much ahead for us as we strive evermore to know your presence in us. In offering our wholeness to each other, we begin to realize your holiness and become one with it. In all of our dreams, we see that we desire only complete union with you. Every pleasure we perceive is an invitation to come into your greatness of being. Let us not become lost in the manifest form of you, but be ever inspired by it to continue on your path.

Lesson: The force overpowers you. You are swept away in an ocean of sensation. Visions totally inspire you. This is a peak experience. You may have to increase your tolerance for bliss. Once again, allow. Let yourself feel the happiness without fear. The wave may subside, but it will rise again.

The illusion is that all future problems are solved by the wave of love you feel. No, this wave has come because you were complete with your past. You fully let go and went ahead. You tied up loose ends and let yourself take some action in your own behalf. When you are current, the current is strong.

So ride this wave. Enjoy it. Live full of grace, but appreciate and be here now. Keep your eye on the present, and continue to give yourself permission to be fully yourself. You did not earn this experience by self-denial. You may deserve it, in your opinion, to balance a previous period of self-denial, but that is not how you got it.

You got it by being you. You had nothing to lose at the time, so you let yourself be. Now continue to live that fully. Be whole. Do not start putting aside parts of yourself for fear they might threaten this wondrous feeling. The feeling is always waiting in the ethers to encompass you when you are courageous enough to be absolutely who you are in the moment. This is an exciting time. Go with it.

Eight of Bowls

EIGHT OF BOWLS:
Journey of Love

Prayer: With the foundation of love that we have built together, we know we can now accept a caring role in the lives of others. Great Spirit, guide us on our way to the fulfillment of our spiritual vessels. We no longer have need of mere pleasures for self alone, but seek to find pleasure as we give love, healing, and service to those who most need our care. Let us know where to serve. We are ready.

Lesson: You have built a solid base from which to take a journey of love and higher exploration. You long for the divine and cannot resist the urge to go ever deeper into this love. You know there is more than human love, and you aim to find it.

It may be tempting to think there is simply a better human to love, but use caution. You are seeking union with a divine force. Do not give up what you have built as your strong human companionship along the sacred way.

It may be time for some changes or adjustment in the relationship, but realize what you have while clearing the way to go on. Seek the eternal. That is all that will satisfy you now. Anything else will at best give temporary pleasure.

Renouncing the world does not mean to have nothing. It means your soul is not possessed by those things around you. Use what you have to liberate yourself from the bondage you feel. Use your inner resources. Reorganize your external environment. The movement you want is internal.

211

Nine of Bowls

NINE OF BOWLS:
Spiritual Family

Prayer: We have believed that love is to give and we have given it. In faith we served as best we knew how. Always, when our bowl was empty, you saw that it was filled once again. Now we are strong in our belief that there is always plenty. We are rich in so many ways. Our love spreads to all we call our spiritual family. Truly, all who live on Earth are our relatives, for they all give to us and all work together in the greater scheme of life. I offer my friends and relations, my children and all creatures, that which you have given me. I have attained the consciousness of oneness. Our interconnections are clear. Guide me now, all the way home.

Lesson: You are beginning to see your relationship to all things. Everything is consciousness in formation. Each tree and flower is a live, sentient being. Every crawling creature, the swimmers, the flyers, the four-leggeds, and the two-leggeds are beings with whom you are in relationship.

You are surrounded by these brothers and sisters who ask you to be involved with them. You are by no means alone. Some are here to serve you in ways you have not yet imagined. You are also here to serve them, perhaps in ways you are just beginning to understand.

We live in a cluttered world of things in the present time. Many of the things are dead in the sense that they have been created without consciousness. They were manufactured without a thought of quality and certainly contain no one's personal energy. These things must steal life from you in order to exist. On the other hand, consider a gift handmade by your child or a clay pot made by a tribal craftsperson as the only cooking vessel for hir family. These gifts are alive with the consciousness of their creator. They enrich your life every time you look at them.

In the cluttered world, you have been taught to ignore many things, things that do not serve your purpose. They are "trash." Trash is a concept of the cluttered world of dead things. Even people have been thought of as disposable and forgotten. Some animals have been deemed worthless and killed. Yet the world continues to increase production of dead things, trash for us to ignore.

You can no longer ignore this waste. The Earth has come alive for you and everything lives. You become friend of the knife that cuts your bread which feeds you. You respect the shovel that digs the hole to plant the grain which is your meal. You feel kindly toward the worm that aerates the soil that feeds the garden that grows your food. And life is suddenly full of friends.

Your bowl is indeed full now. You may want to pass on some of the things you are not currently using—recycle clothes, goods, books—so that you can concentrate on your relationship to those things, animals, and people you really need. Your values have changed.

You are still in the world, but not of the world. The world is a different place to you now. Act to allow yourself time for full relationship with the people and things that most nourish you and with the tools that help you to nourish others.

The boat ride depicted on the nine of Bowls card is a movement away from the idea of separation and toward the understanding that you are in relationship to all that is. Like any relationship to anyone, it is something to be developed and appreciated. It is a richly active thing. There are no longer dead and meaningless parts of life that burden and encumber you. This is a ride to true family and meaningful life.

TEN OF BOWLS:
Your Heart Is Home

Ten of Bowls

Prayer: My heart rejoices, Great Spirit, for I have found the people with whom I am in spiritual harmony, the place to which I am able to make commitment. I celebrate my good fortune. I give thanks for my family of people of like mind. We feel ourselves here to be one with Earth and Spirit. The gifts of these we share together. Bless our ways, and grant that our tribe may continue.

Lesson: Your heart has found its home. Put your full energy into all you love here. Hold nothing back. Your heart has reached the heavens and brought them home to rest. Let yourself feel your commitment to a certain place, a certain community. Love can be expressed very particularly. You have a place to ground all of your high hopes and dreams.

You are going to "do it" now. Longings no longer take you away to the illusive someone or something better. You have reached a time when you must give your full participation to what is before you. Fix it up; make it into your dream. Everything you need for full spiritual growth is here now. Take stock and dig in.

Pull yourself up to the hearth and read Wendell Berry or Robert Frost, maybe Helen and Scott Nearing. These are people with a sense of place. You will now recognize yourself in them.

APPRENTICE OF BOWLS: A Devotion of Joy and Healing

Apprentice of Bowls

Prayer: If I am sick, you heal me. If I am lonely, you send me a friend. If I need to grow, you challenge me. If I am tired, you grant me rest. Great Spirit, I trust in you. I see now that I, too, can be a messenger of hope for others. I can tell them what I have learned and how you have helped me. I will bring your love to the bodies, minds, and hearts of those who need you. I will be a comforter. Your spiritual messengers will be my Guides.

Lesson: All of your time is devoted to love. It does not matter what you are loving, for you have surrounded yourself with things of value and meaning. You appreciate your relationships and spend time improving your ability to communicate the love you feel for each person in your life.

You are learning to be completely immersed in your High Self. Prayers flow as naturally as random thoughts once did. You have formed a personal relationship with an aspect of divinity, perhaps a Guide from inner planes, a saint, or a guru in the outer world. At the least, you have someone within whom you see God and whom you like to emulate.

Your intuition is strong and you want to use it. Go ahead. You are an apprentice, and this is a learning stage. You learn by doing and reviewing. You would not be this far if you had not developed qualities in yourself that you can trust.

There is quite a bit of magic in your life now. Use it always for the greater good. Power is at your command, and you are entrusted, by your spiritual progress thus far, to use it wisely. Your goal is God-realization, not success in worldly terms.

TOTEM OF BOWLS:
Dolphin, the Swimmers

Totem of Bowls

Dolphin
THE SWIMMERS

Prayer: Straightforward I travel, speaking the truth as I know it. I am here not only to console, but to give to others the tools with which they might lift themselves up. I will offer the ideas that free the mind and body and the heart from pain. My life will be lived as an example of harmony and balance among the creatures of Earth. Always, I will seek to live in higher consciousness, the awareness of your presence in all that is. I will act as a warrior on the path of peace. My soul shall be impeccable.

Lesson: Learn from the swimmers. Consider the dolphins, the whales, their patient and persistent love. Go to the ocean or a stream. Float on a still pond. Imagine yourself floating in Great Mother's arms, surrounded by liquid love in the sea of life.

Empty your mind. Let the glistening fish colors, the soft shell shades, the gleaming, subtle rock forms pervade your consciousness. Listen to the sound of water, water creature. Be cleansed. Dissolve all obstacles. Absolve all friendships of any need for guilt. Let go.

Feel your body weightless. Glide. Dive deeper into the pool of love. Watch the sun sparkle on the water until the scene becomes another enchanted world. Play with the waves. See the correlation of all things with your life.

Be a fish. Become at home in the water element. Become at home in the easy push and pull of waves of love. Learn to live as if life were a stream constantly nourishing. Be content in the here and now.

NURTURING LODGE OF THE BOWLS:
The Fruits of Devotion

Prayer: Many things I have been in the world, many roles I have played. Now I rest in the very place where you need me. I know the worldly ways. I have struggled with love and come through smiling. I can tell how each one I have loved has brought me into deeper understanding of you. I see that all of my time has become an ongoing act of devotion to you through all whom I serve. I see that this devotion brings blessings in many forms to my people. Thank you, Grandmother, Grandfather, for the wisdom of your lives you have shared.

Lesson: Enter the lodge of spiritual family and celebrate your lives together. This is the place and time to utilize your stores of nourishment for self and others. Embrace. Be in peace. Reflect. Enjoy.

If you cannot fully do this in your life now, there is a lesson here. You have given away too much, saving nothing for the present. You have extended your hand to others so far that you have lost your balance. Go prepare a nurturing space. Renew yourself. Get what you need to fill your space and feel good about sharing once again with others.

Your life is designed to bring you into constant relationship. Each relationship is a chance to act as if you are serving the Divine Being by serving that part of God that lights each human and creature presence. As you serve God, further God-ness is revealed through each one you serve. Your home becomes your temple where Gods and Goddesses are welcomed and you are able to serve as priest/priestess, host/hostess. All is to be passed on in the gracious ways you have learned. All is meant to be received in thanksgiving and returned, in the end, to Earth itself. This way brings constant nourishment to all who live.

EXEMPLAR OF BOWLS: Ever-Deepening Love

Exemplar of Bowls

Prayer: Only I, an old one, who has raised many children and in them raised the consciousness of the world, can be called Great Grandmother/Grandfather. I have given to all who were young on their road to understanding. I have shared all of my knowledge, all of my poetry, all of my heart's expression. I have loved deeply and long, and I will love you, the newly born living spirit as well. When you do not like yourself, human child, I will say a kind word. When you are lost, I will point the way and let you know you have the feet to walk the road alone. For in all my love, I am strong. I have lived a long time and many lives. From my experience, you will be renewed.

Lesson: Your love has matured. You have many teachings to pass on. Consider how to use your particular talents as

218

a vehicle for the expression of the wisdom you have gained.

It is time for you to settle back and integrate your love experiences. You have reached a plateau. Look back at the far distance you have come. Count your blessings. Bless others with your presence.

You exemplify aging in grace. Your soul is filled with youthful exuberance for life's beauty. Your service to others is as natural as breathing. The light within you radiates fully. The full thrust of your life now goes toward your devotion to higher being.

No anger, pain, guilt, or remorse can hold you down. Emotions are a gently moving sea of bliss uplifting a life of steady devotion to a higher good. You live in the simplicity of right relationship and walk a sacred path. Many friendships embrace you on your way.

You have shown by the example of your loving life a path of liberation from life's problems. Through each one, you have taken the loving action and come through in beauty. Now your life stands as a way others can follow. Your bowls are filled with the treasures of Earth and Heaven. As you continue to pass on these treasures, your bowl will continue to be constantly filled. For all love given, love returns. The Wheel of Life speaks the Law of Love.

Using the Medicine Woman Tarot Deck

Quick Reference Guide: Major Arcana

Before doing any card layouts and readings for yourself or others, it is recommended that you spend at least twenty-two days doing the Major Arcana lessons one by one. Your readings will then be much deeper and more meaningful. After you have spent this time getting acquainted with the Major Arcana teachers, you may use the following quick reference suggestions for each card during the layout and reading process. For more thorough understanding, always refer back to the lesson in the *Guidebook* and do the meditations, affirmations, visualizations, and exercises recommended there.

0 Seed: Plant the seed. Begin. Trust in yourself. Go for it. You cannot see the future from here, but you *can* act on your inspiration.

1 Resources: Your energy is your basic resource. Your sexuality is a large part of your energy system. It involves you in relationship. If you are in a destructive relationship, pick up your power and leave now. Next, look at everything around you. Get rid of the things that interfere with your dreams. Acquire what you need. Be aware, it is probably already at hand. Take stock of your resources and use them wisely.

2 Seeker: Take personal responsibility. Your body is trying to give you a message. Listen to it. Look inside for the answers.

3 Bounty: Nourish yourself. Allow yourself to experience contentment. Gather symbols of past positive experiences to reinforce your feelings of self-worth and stimulate your appreciation of your own experience thus far. Enhance your strong points. Appreciate what you have.

4 Command: You are in a position of power. Take charge. Put your deeply held convictions into action now. Set up a structure that allows this.

5 Peacemaker: Look for your opportunity to make a subtle entry into the minds and hearts of those you want to affect. Timing and way of presentation are of the utmost importance here.

6 Ecstasy: Take pleasure in the heightened sense of well-being you are experiencing now. A balance is taking place within you. Enjoy it.

7 **Warrior:** Celebrate your achievement. You have done your job. Enjoy the results and be willing to allow the victorious moment both its coming and its going.

8 **Healing:** You have worked hard to get where you are. Your system of knowledge can be utilized in this area. Trust your power to mend situations.

9 **Guide:** An inner voice calls you now. As you accept your spiritual apprenticeship, so will you also guide others up the mountain.

10 **Harvest:** You shall reap what you have sown. This is a karmic situation. Do the best you can to release any disappointment. Instead, learn.

11 **Balance:** It is time to restore or replenish something in the larger system of life. Take toward society or the Earth that action which brings greater harmony.

12 **Vision:** Take a complete time out. You are going to see yourself and your life in a whole new way. Do not do anything until you do. A great inspiration is coming.

13 **Sunset:** The old must die to the new. Travel gently across the passing landscape, appreciating all that has been.

14 **Blend:** It is time to integrate the best of the known with the new ideas you are gathering from the unknown. Give yourself time to process your experience.

15 Trickster: Words can fool you. Right now you are tripping over concepts that are hidden behind the surface words you use to describe your present situation. Notice words that cause you to have an emotional response, then examine your underlying beliefs. The cause of your apparent trouble is in a negative idea you hold to be true.

16 Pierced Shield: Long-held attitudes are being challenged and breaking down, but you are not your attitudes. Your higher self is breaking out of its shell. The phoenix rises from the ashes. A greater person is emerging.

17 The Grandfathers: Now, more than ever, a certain history is becoming important to you. Contact sources of ancient wisdom for fresh insight into your life situation. Honor the ways of your Grandfathers.

18 The Grandmothers: It is time to seek wisdom from old wise women. Use the methods of the nature-attuned mothers of Earth for the venture at hand. Follow your body's natural tendencies.

19 Rebirth: A wondrous event is about to occur. Allow your innocent excitement to be expressed. Go ahead and feel your youthful exuberance. Participate fully in this tender moment.

20 Discernment: You have made big changes. Some situations that once satisfied you will no longer feel comfortable. Your attraction to certain people will no longer be as strong. Something deeper compels your energy and attention. You will have to make decisions based on your new priorities. What is really important to you now?

21 Dancer: Act clearly, directly, and immediately. You have viewed the situation wholly. Whatever the outcome, you will benefit.

Mystery, Ritual, and Protection

To people who do not understand the tarot, a reading is a very mysterious process. Indeed, the tarot deals with the Great Mystery, life itself. But the cards, like *everything that exists,* respond only to the energy of the perceivers. Nothing happens to which you do not consciously or unconsciously agree. Reality is constantly created by your thoughts and images as well as by the actions which carry them out. It is fun to treat the tarot, readings, and the deck itself with an attitude of wonder, respecting the awesome forces that underlie all that is. But it is important to remember that the magic is in you and in the universe, visible and invisible, not in the cards alone.

Many people like to use a certain ritual when doing a reading. This serves the purpose of jogging the mind into the frame of reference that they prefer when considering the deeper matters of life. Gypsy rituals, Wicca rituals, Christian rituals, or your own creative rituals are all appropriate. The Medicine Woman deck was conceived especially for people who feel akin to Native American values and rituals, those who love the Earth and want to create a peaceful, ecological future on the planet. All rituals are good if they serve your purposes . . . if they make you high, attuned and in harmony with creation. Use them freely. Some prayers for readings and meditations are offered on the two extra cards of the Medicine Woman Tarot deck.

Sometimes, people like to protect their decks from outside vibrations. Decks can be wrapped in silk or cotton or stored in a wooden box. These natural fibers seem to surround the deck with a pure form of living energy and to keep intact your energy that the deck has absorbed. Other people do not like to have to be so cautious and allow their deck to be freely handled and receive all of life's vibrations from the environment. I suggest that you think this issue over and stick to the way that you prefer. Personally, I like to give my deck, as well as my personal journals, special care and treat them like the important friends they are.

Experiment, enjoy, act . . . for that is life . . . and that is the only way we truly know.

May all your readings be blessed by divine power of the Great Spirit, bringing peace, love, and abundance to you and all whom you serve.

Ho! It is good.

Reading the Cards

There are many formats for laying out and reading tarot cards. Numerous excellent books on the subject are available. Any traditional format can be used with the Medicine Woman deck. I have concentrated on a few unusual layouts that may be of special interest to the Medicine Woman deck users. Oftentimes, it is enough to pull just one card. If you go into its meaning deeply, it can tell you everything you need to know about the question you have asked.

Remember, the cards stimulate your intuition. If you have a strong feeling about what the card means for you, you are probably correct. Learning to trust your own intuition is part of the process of becoming an evolved spiritual being. You may want to write down the meanings that you continuously find one card giving to you if they are different from those in this book. But always try to find the essence of similarity among various interpretations. Sometimes just an unfamiliar word can shift the meaning in your own mind. Restate the card interpretations until the words click for you. In this way, you will always capture the grain of truth in every interpretation and begin to see the underlying principle among all the ways in which a basic lesson of life can be stated.

In preparing for a reading, shuffle the cards until it "feels right." You can cut the cards four times, once for each direction—North, South, East, and West—laying the stacks to the left. Deal from the top. Some people turn each card over from the side to put it face up; others flip the card from the end to face up. Just do it the way that comes naturally to you and always do it the same way.

After laying out the cards, refer to the Major Arcana and Minor Arcana pages for insights and interpretations. The "Quick Reference Guide: The Major Arcana" and the chart "The Minor Arcana: The Four Powers" can also be used.

Major Arcana cards in any position mean that the client is very involved with that issue, and the choices she makes are very important in terms of spiritual growth. Insights and help for making right choices will come from doing the exercises, visualizations and meditations suggested in the pages for that particular Major Arcana card. Also, where a Major Arcana card appears, you may interpret it as that particular archetype trying to contact hir and give hir the gift of its powers.

With Major Arcana, the energy forces at work are greater than the small-self personality level of being. An important step is attempting to be made through the client's being. As she attunes to what that is and what her part can be, she joins the ranks of co-creator with divine forces.

Minor Arcana cards in any position show the general area of life (suits) that the question concerns. They depict possible ways of handling day to day situations. Read, record, or write down the heading that goes with each Minor

Arcana card (for example, Five of Bowls: Letting Go) that comes up in the layout so that the client can take home the seed thought it contains. She can dwell on these few words a couple of times a day, or she can say the prayer that is offered with each card. This will give hir a focus that is oriented toward a positive outcome.

It is especially important, if you are using a deck other than the Medicine Woman deck that you assist the client in finding a positive way to view the image on the card. Many decks are very beautiful, and any deck can be used with *The Medicine Woman Inner Guidebook* and layouts, but some decks contain a few cards with rather frightening images. These can be thought of as "a possible outcome if fear is allowed to rule the situation."

Reversed cards: If a card is laid out upside down, it simply means that the energy or event has, is, or should be taking place on the etheric plane and is not yet in outward manifestation. For instance, a client may have asked if she is going to get a certain job. A reversed card may mean that she does not believe inside herself that she can have this job and should work within, visualizing her success. It could mean, also, that the person in charge has, indeed, decided to hire her but has not yet delivered the message.

Always allow your intuition to help you in interpretations of any card. The cards are tools to help you develop your intuitive knowing. Depend on yourself and encourage your client to depend on herself. The reading is meant to raise ideas of positive potential and to offer encouragement in the direction of actualizing that potential.

A reading can warn of consequences if actions are made in fear, but *a reading never predicts dire consequences.* All reality is fluid and malleable, thus the future *can always be changed* by actions and thought in the present. A reading points out the direction in which the client is presently heading and pattern she is already engaged in (though she may not be aware of the pattern). When the tarot reader offers the cards' interpretation of the future, she is saying, "If you continue in your present vein, this may result. . . . " But the client, on hearing the information, immediately alters the result by her reaction to this prediction and her decisions about it. It is always helpful to discuss these concepts with the client and to arrive intuitively and through discussion at the best possible paths for hir to take.

Negative questions: If the client asks a question in a negative form, such as, "What is keeping me from getting a good job?" she is looking for a block. Interpret the card as the behavior the client is *not* doing. If the card is the eight of Bowls, for example, you would tell hir that she may not be caring for others as much as she could be and that with a little extra effort, things could change dramatically for the better. With a positive question, such as, "What is my best quality?" the eight of Bowls would be interpreted as a strong ability to care for others and to see the divine within them.

Time: When a client wants to know "when" a particular thing will occur, look to the chart "The Minor Arcana: The Four Powers." Pipes are Spring, for example, and an ace of Pipes would be the first week of Spring beginning on the Spring equinox. Twos would be the second week of the season that the suit stands for, on up through Lodges. Exemplar means the matter was completed in that season last year.

You can also look at the card itself to see what psychological process needs to be completed before the event can take place in time. Using the eight of Bowls again as an example, the client would need to do some caring for others before that eighth week of Summer when the event is likely to happen. If the person is blocked in the area that the suit depicts, you can expect a less accurate reading as far as predicting the exact time of things.

The Chakra Tower Layout

A chakra could be said to represent a level of consciousness. The Chakra Tower layout shows where the client is in relation to the issues of each chakra, even if the client has no specific question in that area. This layout also answers specific questions the client may have concerning situations related to each chakra level.

Lay out the cards in a line, one above the other, starting at the bottom. The Tuning Card will be at the bottom, the Seventh Chakra Issues card will be at the top. If there are two questions for one level (chakra), place two cards side by side at that level. The arrangement should be orderly to facilitate the flow of energy in the reading.

Seventh Chakra Issues	Serving the highest good; manifesting vision
Sixth Chakra Issues	Taking charge of thoughts. Pursuing vision. Being seen for who you truly are.
Fifth Chakra Issues	Creativity. Speaking out. Making self known.
Fourth Chakra Issues	Love and romance. Circulation; prosperity. Expanding feelings of relationship to all.
Third Chakra Issues	Personal power. Intellectual ability. Health.

Second Chakra Issues	Kinship; belonging to a group. Feeling accepted and needed by others.
First Chakra Issues	Security, home; safety, self-reliance. Basic sexual energies. Desire for life.
The Tuning Card	Depicts the current feeling state of the client or oneself. If this card is not illustrative of the client's state, do not do the reading right now; something is interfering.

List a question related to the issues of each chakra (level of consciousness). In some areas, you may have two or three questions, but it is better not to try to go beyond this number for any one area (chakra) in a general reading of this kind. If you have many questions dealing with only one issue, use Single Issue Reading.

Single Issue Reading

List all questions relating to the issue the client is working on, but try to stay below about twelve or fifteen questions in all. More than that gives the mind too much to deal with at one time. Arrange the questions in a logical sequence, perhaps in order of priority of importance. Combine questions that seem very similar into one. Number the questions, and lay the cards one after another in a line, circle, or any arrangement that has a good feel to it. Each card corresponds to a question.

The Medicine Wheel Reading

In this simple circular reading, "self" is the client if you are doing a reading for someone else.

Card 1, Self: The center card is always drawn first to show the self as she is at the time of the reading.

Card 2, North: The card placed in the North position will tell you ways to relate to Earth and your material well-being.

Card 3, East: The card placed in the East will tell you how to relate to issues of sexuality, love-partnership, and creative work.

Card 4, South: The card placed in the South will tell you of adjustments you need to make in your thinking in order to fine-tune for the results you desire.

Card 5, West: The card in the West will show you where you can best express your spirituality right now. Devote special time to this, and allow it to become your way to serve higher Being.

Card 6, Evolving self: Pull a sixth card, and place it over the center card. The sixth card shows the self that is evolving as a result of following the requests of the Four Directions.

If you want a particular result in a certain area of your life and want to know how you can achieve this in a holistic way, try this five-card Medicine Wheel Reading.

Card 1, Self: The card in the center depicts the self in relation to that area to which the question refers.

Card 2, North: The card in the North will show a practical step to take. It should be as material as possible.

Card 3, East: The card in the East position will be your inspiration. It is an image to hold in the mind during meditation and should inspire your creativity.

Card 4, South: The card in the South position should be used as an affirmation. Read what the *Medicine Woman Inner Guidebook* has to say about the card and come up with a one-liner that suits your situation. You could also make up a chant or song in order to get these affirming words implanted in your mind.

Card 5, West: The card in the West position will tell you of a movement to take, a way of spending time or of expressing devotion. You may want to do a ceremony that helps you get into the idea behind this card.

What the Medicine Wheel Reading is trying to show you is that there are four areas you must consider in manifesting anything: resources, energy, thought, and movement. You must also allow silence, vision, word, and expression to flow through you in relation to the desired outcome. Nothing is created by desire alone, by material wealth alone, by thought alone, or by action alone. Creation is an integration of the whole.

A Card a Day

Just drawing one card each day is a fine way to focus
energies, especially during trying or chaotic times. The
lessons can then deepen and expand as you see how the
card applies to each different situation of the day.

I recommend using a journal to jot down any personally
meaningful experiences you have with the card. These will
come in handy in future readings you do for yourself. You
are gathering information on the exact meanings each card
has for *you*.

The Final Word

Throughout *The Medicine Woman Inner Guidebook*, I have emphasized your personal power to change your life for the better. You are much more powerful and in control of life than you have been led to believe. I want to encourage you to create the life you want because I believe in you. I believe that your real desires cannot be out of harmony with the good of the whole. But people do not always know their real desires, nor have they been taught ways to discover them. I have dedicated my life to helping them do so. The exercises in this book are designed to get you to the bottom of things going on inside yourself and to raise you to the peaks of experience.

I know we can make a good world. I trust in the divine plan. Yet, I see, too, that people can pick up from writings such as these which emphasize a positive "you can have it all" attitude, that this means they can and should have every frivolous fantasy and worldly trinket. This is not the case. For every thing you take without thought of the giver, whether that be person or planet, you perform an act of greed. Greed destroys you and this planet.

As you seek to have what you feel you can use, create with, enjoy, beautify, and pass on so that others may benefit, your will and the will of the Great Spirit become one. The Mother Earth wishes all her children to have plenty. The divinity within us, male and female, wishes to

235

reach its full expression as God/Goddess by sharing this plenty. You are one with Earth and Spirit, and every action you take affects the whole. I know as you reach into yourself and discover your essence, you will find this to be true.

As you let your true self be all that it can be, the world will be made plentiful again. The direction of the North is, "Go, take my resources, this body of Earth, and make prosperity for all." East inspires us, "Awaken, let your energy form relationship to all that is. Create, and let your creations bless the Earth." South says, "I will give you the courage to continue. Speak in the goodness of your plan as you carry it through." And West asks, "Reflect, look back; this is the completion of your circle. Is your harvest good?" Life continues. According to the will of highest good, God Within, let it be.

To arrange a Medicine Woman workshop in your area, contact the event coordinator at:

The Earth Nation
P.O. Box 929
Nashville, Indiana 47448

Full information is available on request.

About the Author

Carol Bridges was raised in the mystical tradition of the Catholic Church, at an early age communicating with Divine Beings as they were introduced to her by her family and teachers. She was an outwardly quiet child with an inwardly rich and creative life. She later learned that this inner world was called "imagination."

School put a lid on her imagination, allowing it to be expressed only within narrow limitations. But life circumstances and the deep self-reflection she did in response to them eventually caused a death and rebirth experience during the birth of one of her three sons. She awoke after the experience with expanded vision. She was no longer looking at life in terms of her cultural pattern. She had been drawn into a immense field of compassion for all living beings.

While raising three children barely more than a year apart, she began her work to change society. This led her to meetings with many "teachers in disguise" who were able to continue to broaden her perspective and her skills. Her imagination flowered once again, opening up new artistic avenues and causing a more intensive search for the greater truth.

Finding love to be the root of all mystical religious systems, she set about in earnest to learn its ways. She studied psychology, women's issues, and art at the University of Iowa and cast old structures aside to take part in a variety of adventures, including communal living, radical therapy, new relationship modalities and changes in diet and place. Eventually, she found herself to be walking a path worn long ago by native people everywhere.

She had found her spiritual lineage, a blend of East and West, vision and discipline, grounded in the native harmony of the land in which she was given birth and in which she lives this life. Attunement to the Earth around her was the way of her personal past and future. The native way which lives life as art and religion, honoring all being as alive, was the form in which her soul was at home.

Carol now teaches classes and offers workshops and ceremonies through The Church of the Earth Nation in southern Indiana. She is a voice channel for the Guiding Beings and is the author of many articles and books on women's health and spirituality. She has been a sacred teacher at Sun Bear's Medicine Wheel Gathering and is available for consultations and workshops throughout the country.

NOTES

NOTES